britney
spears

britney
spears

Jackie Robb

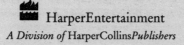
HarperEntertainment
A Division of HarperCollinsPublishers

♛ HarperEntertainment
A Division of HarperCollins*Publishers*
10 East 53rd Street   New York, NY 10022-5299

ISBN 0-06-106620-6

First Edition, 1999

Cover design by Susan and Jeanette
Cover photograph © 1998, Todd Kaplan Star File Photo

Printed in the United States of America

Visit HarperEntertainment on the World Wide Web
at http://www.harpercollins.com

❖ 10 9 8 7 6 5 4 3 2 1

••••••••••••••••••••••••

To Arthur, all my love, "One More Time"

contents

Introduction

Talented, bubbly, bright, energetic, the girl next door and then some—seventeen-year-old Britney Spears is all that and a whole lot more. She's the ultimate pop music princess, whose debut album, ...Baby One More Time, soared to the very top of the music charts. The catchy single of the same name took radio and MTV by storm, and it wasn't long before all of America was happily dancing to her tune. That song brought Britney into the limelight and turned her into an overnight "It" girl—the girl every guy wanted to get to know and every girl wanted to hang out with.

But Britney is also a down-home country girl with confidence, energy, and strong values. She may be riding in the fast-fame lane, but she's definitely remaining true to herself and her beliefs.

From Kentwood, Louisiana, to Orlando, Florida, to New York City, to the world—bouncy, bright, beautiful Britney has been mesmerizing fans with her superhuman voice and her supersweet smile. There isn't a corner of the world that wouldn't be able to sing along to the catchy chorus of ". . . Baby One More Time"—"My loneliness is killing me, I must confess, I still believe. . . ."

Girl singers are certainly nothing new in the pop music biz. Back in the sixties, they sang together in girl groups; in the seventies, they wailed disco tunes. But Britney is most directly descended from two lovable pop music icons of the late eighties, Debbie Gibson and Tiffany. Like them, Britney has a lovable, best-friend quality mixed with heaping helpings of talent and enthusiasm. And also like them, Britney has style and a sense of fun that appeals to fans of all ages.

But Britney's voice—her awesome, powerful, sultry, sophisticated, and ultracool voice—is what really puts her over the top! It's a voice that has been compared with those of the pop divas of our day, like Whitney Houston and Celine Dion. It's a voice that's strong, that gladly tells the world this is one singer who's arrived. It's a voice that can belt out a heart-tugging ballad or a bouncy dance tune with equal conviction and power.

And unlike those untouchable music mavens Whitney and Celine, Britney is still the type of girl you could imagine being close friends with. She's someone you'd love to chat, share secrets, shop, and giggle with, because Britney still does all those things—she's still a teenager, and that means she's always ready to have a good time doing the "girly" things she loves.

Britney may seem like an overnight sensation, but nothing could be further from the truth. She began her career back in her hometown of Kentwood, Louisiana—a seriously small town that specializes in Berry Festivals and beauty pageants. Britney started singing almost as soon as she could talk, and by the age of ten, she was already a *Star Search* Champion and local celebrity. She was also an award-winning gymnast, who spent hours a day perfecting her flips and twists—great preparation for the dance moves she would soon be known for in her hotter-than-hot videos.

At eleven, Britney was starring in the Disney Channel variety show, the *Mickey Mouse Club*, a show that launched the careers of a slew of young stars (including Britney's close buddies Justin Timberlake and J.C. Chasez of the pop-sensational singing group 'N Sync). When the show was canceled, she went back home and lived life as a "normal" teenager. For awhile, at least.

But the bright lights, the screaming fans, and the MTV cameras were out there waiting for her, and Britney was determined to have it all. She pursued her music career, and just after her seventeenth birthday she received a wonderful gift—her album soared to number one! . . . *Baby*

One More Time brought Britney into the big time.

Of course, getting there took hard work. After signing her record deal, Britney traveled the United States, appearing at local malls and bringing her music directly to her fans. Snippets of Britney songs began popping up on the Internet, whetting the appetites of listeners throughout the world. And after the release of her first single, Britney hit the road hard as the opening act for 'N Sync, a concert tour that brought her face-to-face with legions of girls— all ready, willing, and able to dance to the beat of ". . . Baby One More Time." The star herself, always modest and totally unwilling to blow her own horn, was quick to credit the power of pop music, and not her own talent.

"There was this period when everything in music was R&B," she told a popular teen magazine in one of hundreds of interviews she's done over the past year. "Then all the sudden— POP MUSIC! . . . And pop music is fun music— it puts you in a better mood. It makes you happy when you hear it. I know I feel happy when I hear a happy song I can dance and sing along to."

By early 1999, Britney was making millions of fans happy all over the world. She had quickly become one of the most beloved girl singers in pop music history. This sweet and lovely Louisiana girl, who'd always dreamed of hitting the big time with her big, big voice, was a chart-topping, platinum-selling artist. Her concerts were totally sold out, her videos were playing nonstop on MTV, and her face was popping up in magazines and on TV talk shows.

So who, exactly, is Britney Spears? How did this young girl capture the hearts of so many fans, male and female? How did she get her start? And what does her future hold? If you want the answers to these and many other questions, just sit back, get comfortable, and enjoy the read.

chapter one

A Star Is Born!

Britney Jean Spears made her star-studded debut in this world on December 2, 1981. Although her parents, Lynne and Jamie, already had their hands full with their lively five-year-old son, Bryan, they were delighted to welcome their dark-blond, brown-eyed daughter into the family. They spelled her first name B-r-i-t-n-e-y because, as Britney tells it, "My mom said everyone spelled it B-r-i-t-t-a-n-y, but that wasn't how it was pronounced, so she spelled it the way it sounded." They also gave their daughter the middle name of Jean, after Lynne's mother.

Lynne and Jamie brought their bundle of joy home to a Victorian-style ranch house tucked away on a quiet street in Kentwood, Louisiana, about an hour from New Orleans. With a population of 2,500, Kentwood is a place where the birth of a new baby is reason for a total town celebration. Britney remembers Kentwood as a place of simple beauty and old-fashioned goodness. It is quiet, slow-moving, and peaceful, full of serenity and grace. It has a certain old-fashioned timelessness that makes it a great place to be a kid. "It looks like something out of a movie," she told *Tiger Beat* magazine. "Everybody knows everybody. For some reason, all my mother's friends had kids at the same time, so it was like I had all these sisters."

Lynne and Jamie both worked hard to give

their kids the best life possible. Lynne was a teacher, and while baby Britney was growing up, Mom was running a day-care center. Jamie was the foreman of a construction company. When work became scarce near Kentwood, he traveled to Memphis, living there during the week and returning to spend time with his family on weekends.

Life was most excellent for baby Britney—she had a close-knit, loving family (including a big brother who constantly protected her from the world's dangers) and a slew of cousins and neighborhood girls to play with. But she wanted more.

Even at that young age, Ms. Britney Spears wanted the spotlight.

Sing-Along

From the moment she was able to talk, Britney was singing. And from the moment she was able to walk, she was flipping out! "I was crazy," Britney told *SuperTeen* magazine. "My parents' friends would come over to the house, and I would be doing flips across the room. Even then, I loved to perform." Dancing and singing were child's play for Britney, and she did both every single day.

Lynne and Jamie were astounded by their young daughter's voice—it was so strong, it sounded like it was coming from someone three times Britney's age. It was also a good voice—clear as a bell and always in perfect pitch. They encouraged Britney to indulge her love of singing.

One of the places Britney could really let her voice shine was in Sunday services. Britney and her family attended the Baptist Church every week, and she happily lent her voice to the choir. "The church has always been so important in my life," Britney told *16* magazine. "It was the center of our community. And I grew up singing there."

At the age of four, she gave her first public performance, singing "What Child Is This?" for a Christmas service. The audience—fellow parishioners—was awed by her God-given talent.

Despite her young years, Britney recognized the effect her voice had. She saw people turn their heads and listen as she sang; she watched as smiles lit up their faces. She couldn't help but realize that it was she who was making people happy—and the realization delighted her!

The giggly little girl with the voice that could light up a room started school at an early age—by the time Britney was three years old, her mother was already teaching her in the day-care center she ran. By the time Britney entered kindergarten at the Park Lane Academy in Macomb, Mississippi (about thirty minutes from her home in Kentwood), she was already reading at a level higher than her classmates. She progressed well in school—her favorite subjects were spelling and reading. But when she finished her homework at night, she always returned to her first loves, dancing and singing.

It was clear to everyone that Britney loved attention and clamored for the spotlight—but it was also clear that she had the kind of talent that made people want to watch and listen to her. Lynne began to realize that her lovely little daughter had a tremendous voice, a voice that was stronger and more melodic than that of any adult she knew. And Britney's dance moves showed grace and precision far beyond her young years.

As Britney grew, her love of music and performing grew as well. Her occasional bouts of shyness disappeared completely when she was in front of an audience. "I was always dancing in front of the TV," Britney remembers. "My mom would have company, and I'd be dancing and doing flips, and my mom's friends would say, 'Lynne, what's she doin'?' And my mom wouldn't have even noticed me, she was so used to it."

To make the most of Britney's natural gifts, her mom did what millions of parents across the country do for their daughters—she enrolled Britney in dance class. For two years, little Britney devoted herself to learning ballet, jazz, and tap and to performing in reviews and recitals. Lynne drove her daughter back and forth to class in New Orleans and was delighted to see Britney enjoying herself.

But as much fun as Britney was having, she was doing more than enjoying herself—she was dedicating herself to her dancing. She was always pushing herself to learn new steps and was always psyched to show them off once she'd perfected them.

Britney's teachers noticed that she was extremely flexible and strong—capable of doing difficult flips, cartwheels, and summersaults. They suggested to Lynne that Britney pursue gymnastics—she seemed like a natural. Britney jumped at the chance. She started taking lessons and immediately fell in love with it. Although she continued with the dance lessons (and with singing in the church choir), she began to devote herself almost entirely to gymnastics. Before long she was at the top of her class. "Doing gymnastics was so much fun," Britney remembers. "I had the best time doing those flips!"

Taking to the Beam

By the age of seven, Britney had become a serious gymnast and loved every second of it. Her father built her a beam in the middle of the living room, and Britney devoted herself to becoming the best she could be. "I used to cry if I had to miss gymnastics," Britney told *All-Stars* magazine. "My mom would drive me for an hour, one way, to get to gymnastics—she put up with that because she knew how much I loved it."

But while Britney flourished in performance gymnastics, she discovered early on that she did not enjoy the tough, sometimes harsh world of competitive gymnastics. This was particularly apparent when she traveled to Houston, Texas, to study gymnastics with the world-famous coach Bela Karolyi—the man who trained Olympic champions like Kerri Strug. "I went to a meet one time, and there were all these amazing gymnasts, so my dad suggested I try going to their gym," Britney told *16* magazine. "So I went to Bela's camp in Houston and trained there. I started working harder and harder—but by then, I was starting to cry when I had to go to gymnastics. Everyone there was so over the top. I missed the fun of it—I had been good at gymnastics because it was fun, but it got to the point where I didn't want to do it anymore."

It didn't take Britney long to realize that it was time to return to the things that made her happiest—singing and dancing. She recommitted herself to her church choir, where she continued to astound the congregation with her crystal-clear high notes. Without a trainer or anyone else to push her, Britney bloomed on her own—and her majestic voice, so clear and true, grew stronger with every note she sang. It was now evident to everyone in Britney's immediate circle of friends and family that this was one girl who needed to sing the way most kids needed to breathe.

A Regular Kid—Sort Of

If Britney was aware of her precious musical gifts, she didn't make that big a deal about them. She spent most of her spare time with her friends, being a tomboy. "My friends and I all had these go-carts," Britney told *Teen Beat.* "The thing we'd do is, we'd go to this field after it rained, and we'd go mud riding. My mom would get so mad, because we'd come home drenched in mud."

After washing off the mud, Britney would return to her baby-blue bedroom with the white bay window and play with her dolls. And as she played, she dreamed of what she'd be when she grew up. The dream was always the same—she wanted to sing for millions of people and make the whole world smile! She had no idea that in a very short time, her dreams would be "this close" to coming true.

chapter two

Gettin' It Started

By the time she reached her eighth birthday, Britney knew she wanted to pursue a life in music. The question was how to begin. That definitely was not an easy question for a kid from Kentwood, Louisiana, to answer!

Luckily, Britney didn't have to come up with the answer herself—it came to her in the form of another Brit, one of Britney's closest friends from gymnastics. "Brittany's mom had heard about an open call audition for something called the *Mickey Mouse Club,*" Britney told *Teen Machine*. The two Brits begged their moms to drive to Atlanta, where the casting call was being held.

An open casting call for young performers means total pandemonium, and that's just what the girls faced at the studio in Atlanta where the auditions were being held. Hundreds of girls and boys between the ages of ten and seventeen had turned up; many had driven thousands of miles from all over the South. The *Mickey Mouse Club,* which had already been on the air for several years and was a seriously popular show for the Disney Channel, was just the type of opportunity a young performer needed to break into the big time. The show gave its young stars the chance to sing, dance, act in skits, and even do comedy sketches. Britney knew this was where she belonged, and she was determined to make the cut.

She did very well on her first audition—

well enough to make it right down to the wire as one of that day's finalists. At the end of the day, Britney was poised to nab a spot on the *Mickey Mouse Club*. But it was not to be—not this time around at least. "The producers thought I was still too young," Britney told *SuperStars*. "I was so disappointed, I couldn't believe it!"

The producers of the *Mickey Mouse Club* knew that eight-year-old Britney was still too little to keep up with the grueling demands of the show schedule—the youngest cast members at that time were ten and eleven—but they also knew talent when they saw it, and they definitely saw it in Britney Spears. They were not about to let this catch get away.

The producers sat down with Britney and Lynne and began to map out a game plan for Britney's future. First stop, they decreed, must be New York City. They knew of an agent and an entertainment lawyer there who could help Britney take her first baby steps into showbiz.

Lynne was totally floored by the prospect. New York City? What a completely crazy idea! "Where I'm from, you just don't say, 'I'm going to New York,'" Britney told *SuperTeen*. "People were like, 'What are you doing?' It was totally unheard of." So Lynne took her talented daughter back home to Kentwood.

But Britney couldn't stop thinking about New York City and the promise of a music career. Although she continued performing in local talent shows and in the church choir, she felt completely ready to become a show business professional. She kept after her parents, who eventually gave in to their strong-willed and determined child. "I was like, please, Mom, take me! I wanted to go to New York so bad. So I just kept asking my mom and dad, and they believed in me enough to do it. I really wanted to do it, and I was so thankful because they were so supportive. I think they both knew I had this in me," Britney told America Online.

That summer, Lynne and Britney packed their bags and, leaving Jamie and Bryan behind, flew off to the Big Apple. It was their first time in such an enormous, daunting city. It took a while for them to adjust to it. "I thought I was never going to get used to it," Britney remembers. "I was so scared when I first got there. It was like another world to me." But the newness wore off, and soon it was a world young Britney had become very comfortable in.

She's Gonna Live Forever!

Like the characters in the movie *Fame*, Britney began to work full time on her craft. For three summers in a row, she studied at the Professional Performing Arts School (*Home Alone* actor Macaulay Culkin is an alumnus) and at the Dance Center, a well-known Off-

Broadway organization devoted to dance instruction and the arts. Britney and her mom lived in a small New York City apartment, and the family reunited for weekend visits whenever possible.

Although she was still only eight years old, Britney devoted herself to her studies and training. It wasn't long before she made her mark on New York—and as the song says, if you can make it there, you'll make it anywhere.

Britney's big-time dreams finally started to come true when she made it to Off-Broadway. In 1991, she auditioned for and won a role in a comedy called *Ruthless,* based on the 1956 horror film *The Bad Seed.* Britney played Tina, the sweet-faced young thing who is really a ruthless killer run amuck. "It was the hardest thing I've ever done," Britney told *Tiger Beat.* "I was playing the main role, and it was every single night. Plus I was keeping up with my studies. I was really working hard." But for Britney, the payoff was definitely worth it— applause from a live audience. "The show was about this little girl who's really evil," Britney remembers. "I was the little girl—I killed my best friend in the show! It was funny, but in a really sick way. Everybody really seemed to love it."

During that busy time, Britney also worked in commercials, appearing in TV ads for Mitsubishi cars and Malls barbecue sauce, as well as in countless regional commercials. Again she wowed everyone with her professionalism and her talent.

The two years Britney spent working in New York provided her with one of the best learning experiences she could have had, but after six months of working on *Ruthless,* she decided she was ready to pack it in and head home for awhile. "It was Christmas, and I wanted to go home, so I went home," she told *16* magazine.

Oh, Baby, Baby!

Britney returned home to a new role—one she hadn't been preparing for but that she was very excited about: that of big sister. There was a brand-new family addition she was dying to get to know—little Jamie Lyn had been born while Britney was away, and Britney could hardly wait to greet her new sibling. "I always loved taking care of Jamie Lyn," Britney told *Teen Beat.* "It was almost like she was my child, because there's a ten-year age difference, and I always felt protective of her."

After Britney settled in at home and started taking her regular classes at Park Lane Academy, she began attending to some practical matters—like getting a dreaded retainer, a prelude to the braces she later wore. "That retainer was the ugliest thing," she told *16* magazine. "It was like this red thing and had a metallic bottom, and it had a key I had to turn every night, that made the retainer tighter. I lost that thing so many times! I remember I lost it in the cafeteria at school, and it got thrown away—and they dug it out of the garbage can! Later on, when I actually got my braces, I thought they were cool—like I was a real teenager with my metal mouth! But that retainer, that was just gross!"

She's a Star

Although she had just spent two years working in New York City, it would be her home state of Louisiana that would bring Britney her real big break. The long-running TV show *Star Search* was auditioning talent in Baton Rouge, Louisiana, and Britney convinced her mom to take her down. Of course, the show's producers were wowed by Britney's big voice, and she nabbed a spot on the nationally televised show. Lynne left the baby and Bryan with Jamie while she and Britney traveled to Los Angeles, where the show was filmed. Britney was a Junior Vocalist contestant. For the first time, she would be presenting herself and her talent to an audience that numbered in the millions.

Britney, all dolled up in a little black dress with a white lace collar and a huge bow in her blondish-brown curls ("I couldn't believe my mama dressed me up in that outfit!" she told *All-Stars* magazine), had the crowd eating out of her hand as she performed her song. They could hardly believe that enormous, powerful voice was coming out of such a tiny ten-year-old.

The judges agreed that Brit was a singing sensation, and she won her first competition. Unfortunately, the following week she lost the title. But Britney was still a big winner in the eyes of all who heard her singing her heart out. No one who heard her sing would ever forget her.

And Britney would certainly never forget the thrill of performing on TV for a national audience. In fact, the experience got her thinking about a certain Club she still wanted to join!

Aged to Perfection

It was just a few weeks before her eleventh birthday, and Britney was thinking about the *Mickey Mouse Club* again. After all, it had been two whole years since her first audition, and she'd certainly learned a lot since then. She'd starred on the New York stage, and even appeared on (and won) *Star Search*. Perhaps she should take another chance and audition again.

The *Mickey Mouse Club's* producers had not forgotten Britney, and when she auditioned for the show's 1993 TV season, there was no way they were going to let her go again. This bundle of talent was more than ready to face the TV lights and cameras, as well as the live audience that came to cheer on the *Mickey Mouse Club* cast each week. Britney got the job, and once again her mom packed their bags. They moved into a small apartment in Orlando, Florida, not far from Disney's MGM Studios theme park—close enough, in fact, that Lynne could walk her daughter to work every morning! For the next two years, Britney lived her dream—she was a full-fledged member of the Club. There was no stopping her now!

chapter three

Club Kid

B ritney had craved to be a part of the *Mickey Mouse Club* since she was eight years old, and by the time she was eleven, she was ready to grab a pair of Mickey Mouse ears of her own! By the time Britney became a Mouse-keteer (as the Club members were called), the show was already entering its sixth season as one of the Disney Channel's top attractions. It was filmed in front of a live audience at Disney World's MGM Studios, so Britney got to entertain people face-to-face.

The show first aired in 1988, and its concept was simple, fun, and truly entertaining. The premise? Twenty young people, aged eleven to nineteen, from all across America, sing, dance, act in comedy skits, and introduce famous guest stars. The wild and wacky aspect of the show was complemented by a more serious, socially conscious side. Each episode focused on issues that were important to teens, like just saying no to drugs or resisting peer pressure.

Each *Mickey Mouse Club* episode was divided into sections. There was Music Day, where singers like Shai and Brian McKnight would perform. There was Guest Day, where a member of the Club would visit a celeb like Tatyana Ali from *The Fresh Prince of Bel Air* or Jonathan Taylor Thomas from *Home Improvement*. Hall of Fame Day spotlighted the outstanding achievements of everyday kids.

Party Day allowed the Mouseketeers to celebrate special days with themed parties. And What I Wanna Be/See provided viewers with an opportunity to explore career choices and travel to exotic lands. The concept was a hit, and so were the show's talented teenage stars. Audiences tuned in every day to catch a glimpse of the energetic and appealing performers.

In addition to the show, there was also a popular *Mickey Mouse Club* album, which debuted in 1993—the year Britney jumped on board. The album featured twelve original songs by thirteen of the Mouseketeers, and the group planned a ten-city concert tour to publicize their music, which was a mix of R&B, funk, and hip-hop.

Earning Her Ears

Britney debuted on the *Mickey Mouse Club* along with six other newcomers: Christina Aguilera, Nikki DeLoach, T.J. Fantini, Ryan Gosling, Tate Lynche, and Justin Timberlake. (If some of those names sound familiar, there's good reason—check out the enormously successful alumni of the show in the next chapter.)

Britney began to split her time between her home in Kentwood and her new home in Orlando. She also began to train with the show's vocal coach to strengthen her voice and prepare for the arduous schedule of a variety show. "It was a great training ground," Britney told *16* magazine. "We were all like a family. We were all different ages—like from twelve to twenty—and we were all singing and dancing and acting. It was the greatest experience."

The *Mickey Mouse Club* also gave Britney her first taste of national exposure and publicity. As soon as she began appearing on the show she started receiving tons of fan mail, and she began popping up in a variety of magazines for young readers. Her fans learned that (back then) her nickname was Bit-Bit, that she loved Tom Cruise, vanilla ice cream, and the book *Little Women,* and that she had no use for selfish people. She was quoted as saying, "Life is short, don't waste it," and urged fans to "be kind and respectful of others."

Although Britney was still young, she immediately took to performing in front of a live audience again. Her years of gymnastics, singing competitions, and Off-Broadway performances had given her poise and confidence on stage, and she was perfectly comfortable doing anything the script called for, from taking a pratfall in a skit to belting out solos. At a young age, Britney already exhibited the signs of a showbiz professional, ready to learn new things and eager to show off her skills.

She wasn't too professional to play, though! Britney was fascinated by the heavy makeup applied to her face (necessary when you're performing under bright lights). So fascinated, in fact, that she wanted to wear it all the time. "I used to put it on after the show was done filming and ask everyone, 'Do you like my makeup?'" Britney told *Teen Beat*. "I cried when everyone told me I was too young to wear it every day!"

Britney and the rest of the cast also found plenty of fun things to do during their free time—after all, the studio was right in the center of Disney World! "We had such fun in those theme parks," Britney remembers. "It was like living and working in a fantasy world!"

Working for a Living

Life as a Mouseketeer might have been fun for Britney, but it wasn't always easy. The team worked Tuesday through Saturday—as in *all day* Tuesday through Saturday. Britney would wake up at 7 A.M. and catch the van that drove her and her fellow cast members to their special school on the show's back lot. From 9 A.M. to 12:30 P.M., they were tutored (Britney was an ace in social studies and English, but she had to struggle through math class, which she was never particularly crazy about). After school came rehearsals, which would run anywhere from one to three hours, depending on the script and how quickly everyone learned it. Hair, wardrobe, and makeup followed, and by 3:45 P.M., Britney was ready to go on. The show would then be taped—three hours of nonstop performing in front of an audience. After the taping, Britney would head home to eat dinner and do her homework. It was a grueling schedule, but she took to it like a fish to water. "I was learning exactly how much I loved performing," she told *Teen Beat* magazine. "That was when I realized how much I loved to sing."

Since Britney was the youngest Mouse-keteer (along with Christina Aguilera—the two became best friends for the two years they appeared on the show), she admits that she had it a little easier than some of the older kids, who probably felt a lot more pressured to be perfect in front of the camera. "I was the baby," Britney told America Online. "I was eleven, the youngest one on the show, so people catered to me. And goodness, being in Disney World alone was so much fun for me. It was like a dream come true."

The friendships that were formed during the time Brit spent on the *Mickey Mouse Club* were intense, so it's no surprise that when Britney remembers the old days, she sounds just a little sad about losing touch with so many of her old friends. "I hope we all have a reunion some day," she told *Tiger Beat* magazine. "It would be a shame, you know, to think about never seeing those people again. The bonds between us were so strong."

And what about the big rumor surrounding Britney's "young love" with fellow *MMCer*

Justin Timberlake? The two were just eleven when they met and became friends, and they definitely shared some sweet hand-holding moments (and even an innocent smooch or two). But they were not serious. In fact, Justin's real first girlfriend was another cast member named Mindy.

For Britney, her time at the *Mickey Mouse Club* gave her two very important gifts. The first was the experience of a lifetime—the chance to learn new skills and perfect her old ones. The second was proof once again that a life in the spotlight was what she most craved.

Two years after Britney signed on with *MMC*, the show was canceled. And although everyone on the show was disappointed, it would be, for Britney, a major turning point. "After *Mickey Mouse Club*, I decided to go back home to Kentwood and try to just be a regular kid," Britney told *Teen Machine*. But those "regular kid" days would most certainly not last forever.

Britney's *MMC* Stats

One of the many things Britney learned from being on TV was that the audience wants to know everything! Teen magazines were constantly interviewing the young cast of *Mickey Mouse Club*, and Britney was no exception.

Although she was young, Britney had

already developed some strong opinions and definite tastes—and she was completely comfortable about sharing them with everyone. She filled out a fact sheet back in 1993 on which she listed her favorite things.

1. **Color:** *Blue*
2. **TV Show:** *Home Improvement*
3. **Movie:** *The Hand That Rocks The Cradle*
4. **Actors:** *Tom Cruise and Demi Moore*
5. **Singers:** *Whitney Houston*
6. **Food:** *Pizza*
7. **Book:** *Little Women*
8. **Vacation Spot:** *Florida*
9. **Sports Team:** *Chicago Bulls*
10. **Best Day Of Her Life:** *"When I found out I had gotten the Mickey Mouse Club."*

chapter four

The Mickey Mouse Club Hall of Fame

Britney Spears is just one of the *Mickey Mouse Club* alumni whose career really took off after the show ended. A whole bunch of Britney's co-Mouseketeers are currently making names for themselves in different areas of the entertainment world. Check them out.

KERI RUSSELL: *Mickey Mouse Club*'s golden girl, Keri Russell has taken her long mane of dark blond curls and her sweet, sincere smile to the top of the ladder in television. After starring in a short-lived NBC show called *Malibu Shores* in 1996 (a show that was created by *90210*'s Aaron Spelling), Keri soared to superstardom as the lead in a show of her very own, *Felicity.* The show was hyped in a big way months before it hit the airwaves, and when it did, it became clear that Keri had that something special that spells superstar. In January of 1998, Keri won a Golden Globe Award for Best Actress in a TV Drama.

TONY LUCCA: Keri's *MMC* co-star became her *Malibu Shores* co-star—and all the while, the two were a very together, in-love couple. (They'd started dating during their *MMC* days, proving that young love can last!) These days, Tony's staying away from the harsh glare of the TV lights and working on his music—he's a talented singer, musician, and songwriter whose CD can be purchased over the Internet. The pair live together in an apartment in California and are totally happy.

NIKKI DELOACH: Born and raised in Georgia, Nikki grew up singing and was determined to pursue a musical career after leaving *MMC*. She is currently a member of the girl group Innosense (a group Britney almost joined as well). Their debut album will be in record stores soon.

RHONA BENNETT: The gal who hailed from Chicago, Illinois, and wowed audiences with her awesome voice is currently working on her debut album.

RYAN GOSLING: The sweet blond boy with the impish but innocent smile showed up recently on the syndicated hit TV show *Young Hercules*. The show films in New Zealand, so Ryan was away when his former *Mickey Mouse Club* co-star Britney hit it huge. "I knew she was destined for great things," he told *16* magazine.

JOSH ACKERMAN: The bright-eyed, sarcastic, and lovable comedian of the Club, Josh is currently working on his first love, music.

CHRISTINA AGUILERA: One of Britney's closest friends on the Club, Christina shared Brit's ambition and love of music. She recorded the song "Reflections" for the *Mulan* soundtrack and is currently awaiting the release of her own pop album.

J. C. CHASEZ and JUSTIN TIMBERLAKE: The boys are all right and in sync—as in 'N Sync! Justin and J.C. kept in contact after the cancellation of the *Mickey Mouse Club*, and both continued to work on their vocal abilities and dancing techniques. In 1997, when pop music was just beginning to hit its peak again, the guys hooked up with Chris Kirkpatrick, Joey Fatone, and Lance Bass, and the rest is 'N Sync history! J.C. remembers his *Mickey Mouse Club* years with pride. He told *Teen Beat* magazine, "It was the greatest experience, because we all got to do so many things. We sang, we danced, we acted—we even did comedy skits. It taught me so much about performing. Doing a variety show like that was the best experience I could have had. It prepared me for all the hard work and performing that's involved in the music business. I know I'm a better entertainer because of my years on *MMC*." And as for Justin—who, like Britney, was one of the "babies" on the show—he simply remembers, "It was a great time, and I'll never forget a second of it."

In hindsight, the *Mickey Mouse Club* was an amazing show that gave many talented young people the chance to shine for the first time— and obviously not the last. But Britney told *Teen Machine* that she never dreamed she and her co-Mouseketeers would reach such heights of fame. "I was twelve years old then, and it was a total friend thing for me, for everybody," she says. "We never really thought, 'Oh, this person is going to do this, or that person is going to do that.' No one ever said that. We would say, 'I wish you the best of luck' and everything, but we never sat around discussing where we would end up. So it's weird to look back and see how well everyone's done. It's just amazing to think about where we started and where we all are now."

chapter five

Taking a Break Before "The Big Break!"

When the lights went down on the *Mickey Mouse Club,* Britney was thirteen years old and had been performing, in one way or another, almost all of her young life. So when she packed up her *MMC* souvenirs and returned to Kentwood, she wasn't sure how she was going to feel about it. "I thought, I want to be a regular kid," Britney told *SuperTeen* magazine. "I don't want to look back and regret not having done that. But of course it was weird—I'd been away for so long, and I'd been working. It was strange going home again."

So Britney went about the business of being a normal kid. She returned to Park Lane Academy in Mississippi for a year and concentrated on being an all-around average junior high school student. She excelled in some subjects but really had to work at others. "I never had a problem with English and history," Britney recalls. "I mean, you use English all the time, and history is so interesting. But math— no way. I was a total goob at it." Britney also enjoyed the "regular girl" activities she and her friends did as often as possible—going to the movies, shopping, and just hanging out. She also loafed a little. "At home, I could get away with doing nothing," she told a local New Orleans newspaper. "I'd come home from school, watch TV. In the summer, I lay out by the pool." Britney also dated occasionally, and she gossiped with her friends about boys she liked.

The one activity that Britney didn't participate in? Talking on the phone! "I'm not a phone person," she told *16* magazine. "My friends love talking on the phone all day— they'll call me up and ask, 'What are you doin'? What are you watching on TV?' Me, I'd rather talk to someone in person!"

Occasionally, of course, Britney got herself into some trouble. "When I started going out with my girlfriends, my mom would give me a curfew," Britney told *Teen Beat.* "I always thought it was too early! But my dad was always stricter than my mom. One time I remember, there was this guy I really liked. I went to stay at my friend's house, and he came over and we rode into town for awhile. It was my way of getting to go out with him! But when my dad picked me up the next morning he was really angry, and I got punished for that. But it wasn't too bad—I mean, if my parents punished me by taking away the phone, I'd be like, 'OK, I'm not on the phone anyway!'"

In other words, Britney lived a totally normal life.

But after a few months of the normal life, she started to come to some serious realizations. She saw that the normal teenage rites of passage were great, but she still longed for the spotlight. Although she loved spending time with her friends and family, she missed the excitement of working and performing every day. And while she enjoyed sharing secrets with her friends, she found it hard to convey to them just what performing meant to her. Most importantly, she was coming to understand that show business was, to her, more than a childhood hobby—it was a calling, a career that she was destined for, charged by an ambition that was in her blood. "I wasn't happy just hanging around at home," she told *Tiger Beat* magazine. "I wanted to see the world and make music and do all these wonderful things."

Almost Innosense

Around that same time, Britney got word that a girl group was forming down in Orlando, Florida. Nikki DeLoach, her *MMC* co-star and close friend, had already signed on, and Britney was asked if she wanted to try out for it as well. The group would be called Innosense. "I thought it would be a lot of fun to be in a girl group with Nikki," Britney told *16* magazine.

She auditioned in the months just before her fifteenth birthday, and she did very well, but she eventually realized it wasn't for her. "I decided not to do it," she remembers. "The timing was just wrong, because I was still going through my 'regular kid' phase." (The group Innosense did get a record deal, by the way. The girls—Nikki, Mandy Ashford, Danay Ferrer, and Veronica Finn—are managed by Lynn Harless, who happens to be the mom of 'N Sync's Justin Timberlake. Got it?)

Our pop princess is all ears when it comes to her fans. Here she is talking to listeners on a call-in radio show. (©1999, Mark Allan/Alpha/Globe Photos)

Britney warms up to fellow pop superstars 98° at the 1998 Jingle Ball. (©1998, Anthony Cutajar/ London Features)

Life is a bed of roses for the reigning queen of pop...but luckily this hard-working diva's not the type to rest on her laurels for too long.

(© 1999, Mark Allan/Globe Photos)

Live and learn. Britney schools fans in the fine art of pop music. (©1998, Alex Lloyd Gross/ Star File Photo)

The *Mickey Mouse Club* was a crucial stop on Britney's road to fame. (©1993 Courtesy of the *Mickey Mouse Club*)

The rising star helped *Teen People* celebrate its first anniversary in style. (©1999, Steve Granitz/Retna Ltd.)

Britney took her *breakout* album and single all the way to #1 on the *Billboard* charts "*...Baby One More Time*"... (© 1998, Ernie Paniccioli/Retna Ltd.)

...and now she's sitting pretty at the top of the music world. (© 1998, Ernie Paniccioli/ Retna Ltd.)

The teen diva represents at the 1999 American Music Awards.
(©1999, Paul Fenton/Shooting Star)

Here she is again in concert at the Universal Amphitheater in Los Angeles.
(©1999, Jeffrey Mayer/Star File Photo)

Britney pitches in to help with distribution of her monster hit debut CD.
(©1998, Mary Monaco/ Shooting Star)

Brit dishes another danceable tune
to an appreciative London crowd.
(©1999, Mark Allan/Alpha/Globe Photos)

A quick café latte break and it's back to business for the megapowerhouse singer. (©1999, Mark Allan/Alpha/Globe Photos)

The "almost" experience with Innosense, along with her own overwhelming determination to return to the performing life, led Britney to make some serious life-altering decisions. She came to the conclusion that a girl group was not the answer for her—for Britney, it would be a solo career, all the way to the top! "I suddenly realized that's what I wanted," she told *SuperStars* magazine. "And suddenly everything became clear."

Britney ended her high school career and enrolled in a home school program based out of the University of Nebraska. "It's mainly for kids who travel with their parents, who are missionaries," she told *All-Stars* magazine. "I took the prep course, and it was so over my head. I had to get one of my teachers to come and help me, and my answers on the prep test were still wrong. It was so hard, oh my goodness!"

But the home schooling was necessary because Britney was on a musical mission, and she definitely didn't have time to do the regular school grind. She was busy every day, preparing demo tapes she would eventually send to Jive Records, the company that signed her. Every single afternoon she would sing into her tape recorder, dreaming of the time when she could use that tape to get a record deal of her own.

Although Britney would never regret taking a year off to pursue a normal teenage life, she admits that for her it got old very quickly. "I got really, really bored," she told *Teen Machine*. "I just wanted to perform again." Britney would get her wish, but it would take a lot of work and a lot of determination—and fifteen-year-old Britney was totally ready for it.

chapter six

Time to Make the Music

All the years of working within the entertainment industry paid off for Britney when she decided to pursue her solo music career because she knew exactly how to go about it. The question remained: Was the world ready for her powerful pipes and over-the-top energy?

The answer would prove to be a resounding yes! By the time Britney made her move, pop music—the kind Britney loved and wanted desperately to make—was high on the charts again. Grunge, alternative, and rap music had dominated the charts for years, but now peppy pop tunes—like those sung by Hanson, the Spice Girls, and the Backstreet Boys—were returning to radio in a big way. The timing could not have been better.

And that's what Britney's entertainment lawyer, Larry Rudolph, told her dad when the two first talked about building a career for Britney. (Larry had known Britney since her days in New York City.) "Larry told my father that pop music was coming back," Britney told *Entertainment Weekly*. "He told me to make a tape and send it to him."

Britney gathered up the precious demo tape she'd been recording, put it into an envelope along with a photo of herself, and sent it on to Larry—who knew immediately that Britney had the talent to make it to the top. He could see she had a great look, and after listening to the demo tape, he knew she had the perfect sound. He brought the tape and the picture to Jive Records in New York City. Everyone at Jive agreed—this girl had it goin' on!

But the tape was only an introduction—the executives at Jive needed to meet Britney to make sure she could really sing, that the tape they'd heard didn't use technical tricks to enhance her soulful voice. Soon Britney was back in the Big Apple to audition in person for the creative staff at Jive Records. "I went there with this dinky little tape," she told *Billboard* magazine. "I felt so weird, standing in a conference room, basically singing for my life. But you have to take whatever opportunities come your way and make the most of them."

As usual, Britney made the most of her golden opportunity. She sang her heart out, and again her audience—this time made up of record executives—couldn't believe what they heard. They signed Britney immediately. She was ecstatic. "I thought, this was too good to be true!" she told *Entertainment Weekly*.

Jive's Talkin'

Teaming up with Jive Records was the smartest thing Britney could possibly have done. The label had built a strong reputation guiding the career of the Backstreet Boys: It had spent well over three years putting together the group's awesome self-titled debut CD, which had reached platinum seven times around the world. Jive Records was the company that had helped Kevin Richardson, Howie Dorough, Brian Littrell, A.J. McLean, and Nick Carter become international superstars, and they were certainly in a position to help Britney achieve the same success.

Jive Records' senior vice president of Artists & Repertoire, Jeff Fenster, was confident that Britney had the right stuff. "Her vocal ability caught me right away," he told *Billboard* magazine. Now it was his job to team Britney up with producers and writers who could use that vocal ability to make the most beautiful music imaginable.

The Sweep to Sweden

Although those outside the pop music world might not know it, Sweden has become an international mecca for recording studios. The pop group 'N Sync recorded their debut album there, and the Backstreet Boys did some work there as well. It was decided that Britney would record most of her album there, then return to New York to work on postproduction.

Britney flew to Sweden to meet with legendary producer and writer Eric Foster White, who'd created musical magic for artists like Boyzone and Whitney Houston. Together with Sweden's Cheiron Productions team— producer Max Martin (who'd worked extensively with the Backstreet Boys) and Per

Magnusson—Eric wrote the songs that would appear on ... *Baby One More Time*.

Jive's Jeff Fenster took the trip with Britney, and together the entire creative team began working on the album. Everyone was impressed with how quickly the recording sessions sped by—most of it was finished in an astounding ten days. "They came up with such incredible stuff," Jeff told *Billboard* magazine. "It came together so quickly for a pop album. It was a case of good chemistry among a group of very talented people."

Britney was especially psyched when she realized that most of the recording would take place in the studio Eric Foster White had built in his own home. "It was so comfortable," she told *16* magazine. "It was hard work, but we always took the time to goof around and act stupid." That comfort level was important to Britney, who was confident, but nervous about working with such major music players.

Getting Inspired

The star-to-be was caught in a total whirlwind of work—every day she went into the studio and gave her music everything she had. Every night she went home and fell soundly asleep. Although the experience was intense, it energized her. Working with such talented writers inspired her to write her own songs—something she'd never done before.

Although Britney did not write any of the songs on her first album, she hopes some of her tunes will appear on future records. In fact, the very first song she wrote, "I'm So Curious," will be on the B-side of her next single. It's a song she loves—and you'll never guess how she wrote it! "I don't really have time to sit down and write," she told *Tiger Beat* magazine. "But when I think of a melody, I call up my answering machine and sing it, so I won't forget it. Then I press play and hear myself singing the song!"

New York Bound

After putting down her vocal tracks, Britney got back on a plane and returned to New York, where the final recording sessions took place. She was thrilled to be back in the Big Apple. "Every time I'm away, I just can't wait to be back," said Britney of her adopted hometown. "I love being in the city—although the taxi drivers make me nervous. When I'm in the backseat of a taxi, I just close my eyes!"

While the final work was being done on the album, Britney got a chance to enjoy herself. She indulged in her love of Southern food, eating at Virgil's Restaurant ("It's got the best cheese grits!"); she shopped and attended dance class regularly. She quickly got used to the frantic city pace and fell in love with it. Country girl Britney was slowly becoming a citizen of the world. New York City would be just the beginning.

Ready or Not!

In mid-1998, everyone involved with Britney's debut album gave it a listen and realized they had a serious hit on their hands. But recording the album was simple compared with what came next—getting people to listen to it by promoting it around the world. Was Britney up to the challenge?

chapter seven

Jet-Setting the World on Fire

In June of 1998, the world got its first earful of pop princess Britney Spears—and everyone loved what they heard!

To build momentum and generate media interest and public awareness of the CD, Jive Records carefully put together a plan to get the word out about Britney's debut album.

The first thing the record company did was set up a toll-free number so that both established and potential fans could call in and listen to snippets of the music as well as to interviews with the star herself. They put the telephone number on a series of postcards, which were then sent to members of other pop music artists' fan clubs, such as the Backstreet Boys Fan Club. The promotion worked like a charm—people who called in to hear Britney's music were intrigued. They couldn't wait to hear more.

Next, Jive Records jumped into cyberland. They set up a World Wide Web Page that featured pictures, interviews, and even more music clips. Fans in the United States were just beginning to get to know Britney, and the response was enthusiastic. They seemed especially taken with the catchy, not-to-be-forgotten ". . . Baby One More Time," which was slated to be Britney's first single. "People seemed to really love that song," Britney told

Teen Beat. "Everyone thought that one was going to do really well."

Flying Far and Wide

If Britney thought she could take a rest after recording the CD, she was mistaken. The time had come for the really hard work!

To promote her album, Britney flew to Singapore. That might seem to be an odd choice for a young pop artist's first promotional concert, but in actuality it was a smart one. Singapore—all of Asia, really—is extremely open to popular music and totally into American culture, so it was the perfect place to launch Britney-mania.

Britney gave her first live concert there and came away from it invigorated and excited. The audiences screamed out her name and danced along to her music—even though many were hearing it for the first time! They loved Britney, and she returned that sentiment. "Oh my goodness, I was so nervous, because it was my first perfor mance," she told *Teen Machine* magazine. "But it was nice. Such a beautiful place. It was so hot outside—it was so muggy, you had to take five showers a day. But it was just perfect. The people and the country were beautiful." To this day, Britney names Singapore as one of her favorite places in the world—she especially loved the shopping! Performing in

Singapore marked a brilliant beginning to what was turning into a brilliant career. Britney had proved she could take the world by storm—but could she hold her own in her own backyard?

chapter eight

Hittin'
the Road

ritney returned to the United States after her exciting concert appearances in Singapore and immediately began another road trip—the homegrown kind! Three months before the release of the single ". . . Baby One More Time," Britney began an intense mall tour of middle America. With two dancers to back her up (and to help her pass out free cassette samplers to all in attendance), Britney set off on a twenty-eight-day jaunt that was sponsored by *YM, Teen, Seventeen,* and *Teen People* magazines. But before she could start her trip, there was one last thing she needed to do.

Her mom, Lynne, had been doing a lot of the traveling with Britney. But they had been told that the upcoming months would be grueling, and Lynne felt she couldn't go out on the road with little Jamie Lyn, who'd just turned seven. "It wasn't fair to make a seven-year-old travel around the world and not have a normal life," Britney told *SuperStars* magazine. "My mom knew she had to stay home and take care of Jamie Lyn, so we had to come up with a plan."

Enter Felicia Culotta, a close friend of Lynn's. "I had moved to New York and was a nanny," Felicia explained to *16* magazine. "After I'd been working at the same place for two years, I figured it was time for a change, and on the very weekend I made that decision, Lynne came to New York with Britney for a meeting with the record company. We all had dinner together, and Lynne said, 'We have a proposition for you! We need someone to take care of Britney.' So it all worked out perfectly!" Felicia took on the responsibility and started traveling with Britney as her guardian. (Lots of fans already know Felicia—she plays the teacher in Britney's ". . . Baby One More Time" video, and she's at absolutely every concert and public appearance.)

With Felicia in place as her caretaker, Britney was ready to hit the road, and hit the malls!

Shop 'n' Sing

Britney's mall tour was a smashing success in every way. As she toured throughout the Midwest, she got a chance to perfect her stage show, integrating precise, eye-catching choreography with her pumped-up pop sound. She also learned a lot about the intensity of a bus tour—the long hours, the lack of sleep, endless movies on the VCR, and days away from home and family. "The only downside to all this is being away from your family," Britney told *Teen Beat* magazine. "Luckily my family is so close, we really bond." To beat the homesick blues, Britney stayed plugged in to her cell phone, which never leaves her side. "I don't even want to know how much money I spent on phone calls home!" she says. "I just call up my mom and say, 'Mama, what are you doin'?' I don't care what time of day it is, I just want to hear her voice."

Of course the mall tour had one or two embarrassing moments along the way. One major one still makes Britney laugh and blush. "The thing was, I was getting ready to perform '. . . Baby One More Time,' which was the last song," she told *Tiger Beat* magazine. "And I was on the stage, and my headset fell off, which is not good at all. Then, another time, I have this big costume I wear at the beginning of the show, where I look like one of the dancers. It's got Velcro on it, and when I start singing it comes off, and I have my performing costume on underneath. Well one day, it decides not to come off! I'm stuck in there, and the dancers are pulling and pulling. I could hear them saying to each other, 'OK, we've got to keep pulling it off,' and I tried to help them, but I was stuck in the Velcro. That was definitely embarrassing."

But aside from those few crazy moments, the mall tour was an excellent experience for Britney. And it was an extra special experience for those fans who got an early glimpse of a superstar on the way to the top. Already the buzz was in the air, and the audience members who hummed along to Britney's tunes were carrying the message—this was the girl to watch!

Radio, Radio

Still, Britney had more than her fans to please. She also had to make an impression on the radio executives who decide what gets played on the airwaves. Most DJs thought Britney's single was super—they recognized ". . . Baby One More Time" as an instant hit. Andrew Jaye of WEOW in Key West, Florida, was quoted in *Billboard* magazine as saying, "It's got one of those 'I can't get it out of my head' hooks that makes you want to go out and dance." Clarke Ingram of WPXY in Rochester, New York, agreed, and added, "Even after hundreds of spins, it's unshakable. Our listeners simply can't get enough of it."

What impressed the radio bigwigs—besides the awesome song, of course—was Britney's sweet but sincerely go-get-'em personality. "Britney shook the hand of every radio programmer in the country," said Jack Satter, Jive Records' senior vice president of pop production. "She's a charming performer and she had a great record to sell."

With pop radio stations firmly in her corner, Britney was positioned for success. Now all the radio world needed was a hit single—and one was definitely on its way!

chapter nine

The Song and the Video

Britney's first single, ". . . Baby One More Time," was released to radio stations on November 3, 1998, and was immediately embraced by the industry and the listening public alike. All the planning, all the hard work, and all the mall touring had stirred music lovers' anticipation. By the time the single hit the airwaves, the world was ready to embrace Britney's first musical offering and usher it right up the charts. The song, which so many fans and fans-to-be had sampled over the Internet, was taking the world by storm.

The single scored higher on the *Billboard* music charts than any other song released that week, including tunes by Alanis Morissette and Goo Goo Dolls. Top Forty radio stations across the country rushed to add it to their playlists.

With its hypnotic beat and catchy lyrics, ". . . Baby One More Time" immediately became a fan favorite. No one was immune to it—before long, everyone was humming it. "Everyone who hears it loves it," Britney told *Teen Beat* magazine. "It's total attitude—I love it a lot."

Within a month—and right on her seventeenth birthday—". . . Baby One More Time" slid up the *Billboard* Hot 100 Music Chart into the number nine position. It also hit number six on *Soundscan*. "I heard all about this on my birthday," Britney told *Tiger Beat* magazine. "So we all went out to a restaurant and had a big birthday cake—I was so wrapped up in my birthday, I didn't even focus on how well the single was doing."

Soon there was even more reason to celebrate. By the time Christmas 1998 rolled around, ". . . Baby One More Time" had jumped to number four on *Billboard's* Hot 100 and on *Radio & Records* CHR/Pop Chart. Then, on December 28, Britney was told her single had gone gold—more than 600,000 copies of the single had been sold. (The song eventually sold more than 900,000 copies.) Britney was so excited, she felt she was going to bust. "It's so neat, it's just crazy, isn't it?" she enthused. "I'm so happy and so thankful—but this is crazy!"

Britney went even crazier when she heard the single on the radio for the first time. "I was home, I'd just gotten off an airplane, and I was in the car heading home, when—oh my goodness!—it came on. It was so weird. I started screaming like a big goob."

A Picture's Worth a Thousand Words

Meanwhile, the video for ". . . Baby One More Time" was steamrolling every major video outlet. Shot in Los Angeles with director Nigel Dick (who also directed videos for the Backstreet Boys, Oasis, and Savage Garden), the video shows Brit dolled up in a schoolgirl's uniform, singing and dancing up a storm. According to Nigel, his job was "to bring life, fun, and color to the video." He did all that and a whole lot more.

The video, which was shot at Venice High School (the school that provided the backdrop of Rydell High in the movie *Grease*), was provocative and sexy, but more importantly it was energetic and filled with life. "I wanted something teenagers could relate to," Britney said. "Something like high school." Kim Kaiman, Jive Records' director of marketing, agreed thoroughly. "Kids love this video. It feels real and it's fun."

Both kids and adults respond well to the video—the cool dancing and the hot music make it a favorite with everyone. Soon, girls began to dress in the style of Britney's video costume. They wore short school uniform skirts, pigtails, and pom-poms and they started showing up at all Britney's live appearances.

The video for ". . . Baby One More Time" was quickly added to active rotation on MTV and The Box, becoming an immediate fan favorite. MTV's senior programmer Tom Calderone hit the mark when he told the *New York Post*, "Britney has star power."

That star power was equally apparent to modeling agencies. Shortly after the release of the video, they began calling Britney in droves, urging the fresh-faced teenager to take the leap into a modeling career. Britney soon announced that she had joined forces with fashion designer

Tommy Hilfiger and that she would be featured prominently in his spring fashion campaign. "I'm a Tommy Girl now," Britney told the *Times-Picayune*.

All the attention might have blown away someone less modest and grounded, but Britney remained her usual sweet self—although she did reveal her determination and her very strong career ambitions. "I've been working toward this moment for a long time," she told *Billboard* magazine. "I just want to keep on building and building."

Road Trip

With radio and video airplay, Britney was fast becoming a major recognizable face in the music field. The media helped, putting Britney's signature smile in every national magazine. Publications like *16, Teen Beat, Tiger Beat,* and *SuperTeen* (which had recognized Britney's appeal early on) started the wave, and it wasn't long before *Teen People, YM,* and *Seventeen* followed suit. Then came the heavy hitters—*Entertainment Weekly, USA Today,* and newspapers in major cities across the country ran huge articles on the gal from Kentwood. Suddenly the fans really began to take notice. "I'd be at a mall, and people would come up to me and ask, 'Are you Britney Spears?'" she told *All-Stars* magazine. And at an MTV appearance in New York City, the fans went wild—girls dressed up in the school uniform outfit, and guys held up signs that read, "I love you, Britney!" and "Will you go to the prom with me?"

Britney had had some experience with adoring fans on her mall tour, but nothing had prepared her for the insanity and pandemonium that her appearances incited among fans now that her single and video were such huge hits. "It's weird, because the guys in 'N Sync can't go out without a bodyguard—fans would do anything to meet them and to touch them," she told *SuperTeen* magazine. "It's unreal." Now the unreality was hitting Britney as well.

As Britney tells it, fame and fans are amazing things—but some people don't understand that Britney needs her privacy like everyone else. "I was at home, and this guy came up to my house," Britney recalled. "I didn't know who he was, and he kept asking people, 'Is Britney home?' It freaked me out so much, I slept with my mama that night! We had to get our phone number changed because so many creepy people like him were calling. And this guy, he knew who my neighbors were—that was just freaky!"

Luckily, most of Britney's experiences with fans have been totally cool. "With me, it's a friend thing," she explains. "Most fans are able to just come up to me and start talking about whatever is on their minds. And that's just fine with me."

'N the Groove with 'N Sync

While the attention from fans was flattering, Britney longed to get back in front of an audience, to recapture the energy and feel the rush of performing. It seemed that a major tour across the country was definitely in order.

Enter 'N Sync. The awesomely popular boy group, which had taken America by storm with their smash hit singles "Tearin' Up My Heart" and "I Want You Back," were touring the country during the fall of 1998. Britney was quickly signed on as the opening act—a role she took on with some trepidation. "It's not easy being an opening act for these guys," she told *Billboard* magazine. "There are all these girls in the audience, and they're all there to see 'N Sync. But ultimately I'm able to win them over. I have guy dancers, and believe me, that helps."

Britney knew about opening acts from her own experience as an audience member. "I've been to see the Backstreet Boys in concert," Britney explained to *SuperTeen* magazine. "And that crowd is there to see the Backstreet Boys, and they're chanting for them. I thought, 'Oh no, I'm gonna die if I get up there and that happens to me!' But luckily, the timing was good for me because everyone knew '. . . Baby One More Time' from the radio. So I was able to look out and see people singing along—it was really cool!"

Of course, the tour also reunited Britney

with her former *Mickey Mouse Club* friends
Justin Timberlake and J.C. Chasez, who'd found
the monumental success they'd always dreamed
of. Britney was psyched to be traveling with
friends, and she felt their *MMC* connection
broke the ice and made her feel more
comfortable with 'N Syncers Lance Bass, Chris
Kirkpatrick, and Joey Fatone.

It took Britney only a few days to get accus-
tomed to the mind-bending (and backbreaking)
schedule of a national tour. "The first week was
really weird," she told *Teen Beat* magazine. "You
have to get adjusted to being on a bus and not
getting much sleep. But once I got used to it, I
loved it. I love being on the road."

Fans flocked to the concerts, and although
many may have been there only to swoon over
'N Sync, most were totally in Britney's corner,
singing along with her when she belted out
". . . Baby One More Time." "The timing was
good, and the song was still doing well on the
radio," Britney explained to *All-Stars* magazine.
"It was the best feeling, to look out into the
audience and see them singing along with me."

On the Road Romance?

While Britney was on the road with 'N Sync,
a curious rumor sprang up that she and Justin
were a romantic item. Despite Britney's protests
to the contrary, the rumor continued to grow
and spread. "Girls sometimes send me letters

saying, 'Stay away from my man Justin,'" Britney revealed to *16* magazine. "And I'm like, no problem. The guys in 'N Sync are just like big brothers to me. They're very sweet and supportive, but we're really just friends."

But it soon became clear that Britney and Justin were more than just friends. The tabloid newspaper *The Star* reported that the pair were indeed involved in a romance. "I can't believe I'm in the tabloids!" Britney joked when asked about the article—but she did not deny that she and Justin were an item!

Only time will tell if this teenage love connection will continue, but for now, with both Britney and Justin concentrating on their careers, you can be sure it's more often than not a long-distance romance. More than anything, Britney sees Justin as a true friend she can share her experiences with. "The most important thing in any relationship is truth and honesty, and to be able to talk about your feelings," she told *Teen Beat*. "The jealousy thing—that can be a problem. In this business, your friends and boyfriends have to understand how hard you work every day. It isn't all fun and games." Obviously Justin knows a thing or two about that!

Workin' It on the Road

The tour solidified Britney's position as pop princess among her fans. It also helped her develop her performance skills and sharpened her ability to think on her feet. "One time I was on stage and there was a cupcake on the stage, and I was dancing and getting all into it, and I stepped on the cupcake and slipped and fell," Britney told America Online. "There I was, sitting on my butt in the middle of the stage! I had to pretend everything was fine, that it was all a part of the act."

With her four dancers—T.J., Andre, Carissa, and Tonya—Britney and her choreographer, Fatima (who does all the choreography for the Backstreet Boys), were able to create a visually appealing stage show filled with energy and spirit. Britney's dance background made learning the steps a little easier. "In the beginning I was so nervous," she remembers. "But once you start doing it, it becomes second nature, and all that nervous energy helps keep you pumped and moving on stage."

And each night before Britney took to the stage, she had a preshow ritual that kept her grounded and focused. "We all of us get into a circle and say a prayer before each show," she told *Teen Beat* magazine. "God is very important in my life. It's bad because, with all the touring, I don't get to go to church. But I have my prayer book every night, and on the road I always say my prayer before every performance." Britney's faith is of major importance to her. She always wears a band around her wrist engraved W.W.J.D.?—"What would Jesus do?"

Life on the Bus

Hitting the road and touring the country means spending long hours in a tour bus—but bubbly Britney quickly came to think of her tour bus as a second home. "Me and all my dancers ride the bus together, and we act like total goobs," says Britney. "We watch so many movies and we goof around so much."

But as Britney says, it isn't all fun and games. She was pensive when she told *Teen Machine* magazine, "Sometimes I can't sleep, or we get in really late and there's an interview the next morning at six. The worst part of this lifestyle is definitely not getting enough sleep."

... Tomorrow the World

The Britney juggernaut shows no sign of slowing down any time soon. In fact, it looks as if the pace will intensify, with Brit taking her live show to Canada, Germany, France, England, and Germany. And this time, Britney will be the headlining, rather than the opening act.

To help her create an awesome live concert, Britney brought in Johnny Wright, who's currently managing 'N Sync. "I saw her perform, and I was so impressed with her," Johnny told *Entertainment Weekly*. "I'm going to be involved with all her touring and all her live performances. She's basically got all the ideas, I'm just there to help her."

Britney was delighted that Johnny—who's

had tons of experience working with pop performers, including the legendary New Kids On The Block—was on her team. "He'd worked so hard with 'N Sync, and you can tell from the shows they put on what a great job he does," Britney told *16* magazine. "Johnny knows what the audience wants to see."

Working with Johnny means that Britney will be returning to Orlando to live for a while—Orlando, Florida, is Johnny's home base. "I'll have to start rehearsing soon for my tour," she told *Teen Beat.* "I'll live in an apartment or a hotel for a few months—but I definitely need to be in Orlando more because I'll be working directly with Johnny."

With all those hands to help her, there's no doubt Britney is completely ready to tackle any new frontier.

chapter ten

Let's Hear It One More Time!

Britney's debut album, . . . *Baby One More Time*, was released to radio stations and record stores on January 13, 1999, and fueled by the high energy and enthusiasm of the first single, the album soared to number one on the *Billboard* charts. Britney's army of fans had their say in a big way. They guaranteed that the success of her CD would be phenomenal.

The album remained at number one for only a week, then dropped, but within four weeks it was back at number one, smashing the nearest competition (*The Miseducation of Lauryn Hill*) by a whopping 70,000 units. With momentum like that, it wasn't long before Britney's monster hit album was selling double and triple platinum.

And the critics, for once, seemed to agree with the opinion of the fans. *Billboard* magazine called Britney's debut, "a Top 40–ready workout filled with hook-laden songs." They described Brit as a girl who'd been "blessed with a sweet voice," and said her music had "hit a nerve among a teen fan base." Finally, they deemed her "a talent to watch."

According to *Entertainment Weekly*, "this seventeen-year-old ex-Disney princess sounds so soulful and Whitney Houston–assured, it's downright scary."

And the national newspaper *USA Today* raved, "Britney is the first star of 1999's new teen-star crop, and she brings a fresh-faced, girl-next-door appeal."

Of course Britney's fans, who had been rooting for her since the release of the single ". . . Baby One More Time," already knew that Britney had it going on musically. And those same fans couldn't wait to plunk down their money to bring home Britney's CD and share her fun, energetic, "soda-pop" world. As Britney herself told *SuperTeen* magazine, "A lot of the songs deal with love and relationships, but there's one song called 'Soda Pop' which is just a happy, party song."

Since Britney is still a young artist, and since this is her first CD, she didn't have the opportunity to write any of the songs (many artists record songs chosen by their album's producer). But she definitely let her voice be heard when the songs were chosen. "I like a song you can listen to, and it changes," she told *Teen Beat.* "I like songs that you can listen to over and over again, and it always sounds a little different."

In the future, Britney will have an opportunity to write her own songs—something she's already begun doing, and doing well. Her first song, "I'm So Curious," appears on the B-side of her single "Sometimes," and Britney could not be happier about that. "When I first got signed to the record label, there were producers left and right, bringing me songs,"

Britney told *16*. "But all along, I was writing on my own, and 'I'm So Curious' was the first one I showed everyone." Britney also explained how the idea for "I'm So Curious" came to her. "It's all about a girl and a guy, and he likes her and she likes him, but she doesn't know if she should go for it and ask him out. So she says, 'I'm so curious'—like about how this is all going to turn out."

Whether she's writing the songs or singing them, one thing is totally clear—with her debut CD, Britney was able to achieve one of her most cherished musical goals. "I hope my album will make people happy," she told *16*. "I hope that when people hear my music on the radio, it'll make their day a little brighter."

. . . *Baby One More Time* Makes the Grade!

The tracks on Britney's album touch on universal themes and ideas that everyone can relate to: love, boyfriends, dating, broken hearts, and bouncing back after taking a fall. But Britney also knows that girls just want to have fun, and many of the songs are a salute to good times, friends, dancing, and just plain partying.

Here's the "inside track" on . . . *Baby One More Time*—and our "making the grade" reviews of each totally toe-tapping tune.

• • • • • • • • • • • • • • • • • • •

TRACK 1: "…Baby One More Time"
Written By: Max Martin
Produced By: Max Martin and Rami in Stockholm, Sweden
Tempo: Definitely up-tempo, a dance tune to the max.
What's It All About: A girl who hopes to get back together with the guy who left her.
What Brit Says: "This song has a lot of attitude. It's got a great beat, and everyone who hears it, loves it."
Grade: A+++ A totally danceable tune with surprisingly moving lyrics. And a catchy chorus definitely doesn't hurt.

• • • • • • • • • • • • • • • • • • •

TRACK 2: "(You Drive Me) Crazy"
Written By: Jorgen Elofsson
Produced By: Per Magnusson, David Kreuger, and Max Martin in Stockholm, Sweden
Tempo: Mid-tempo, a fun song to tap your foot to.
What's It All About: A girl who's so psyched about her boyfriend, she stays up all night thinking about him.
What Brit Says: "I think everyone knows what the girl in the song is feeling. She just can't stop thinking about, talking about, and dreaming about her boyfriend. She's gone a little 'crazy' in a way, but in a good way."

Grade: A This is a total dance song with lyrics that everyone can truly identify with.

• •

TRACK 3: "SOMETIMES"
Written By: Jorgen Elofsson
Produced By: Per Magnusson and David Kreuger in Stockholm, Sweden
Tempo: Power ballad, with emotion to spare.
What's It All About: A young lady reveals her "sometimes" hidden side to the boy she loves, and lets him know that eventually he'll learn all there is to know about her.
What Brit Says: "I'm really glad they decided to release this song as a single. It's very special and I think everyone will really take something from it."
Grade: A+++ This song, which is the second single release from the CD, is a sweet, gentle love song that'll also keep your head bopping in time to the music. The beat may keep you moving, but the heartfelt lyrics will really touch your heart.

• •

TRACK 4: "SODA POP"
Written By: Mikey Bassie and Eric Foster White
Produced By: Eric Foster White in New York City, NY
Tempo: Up-tempo, a soda pop bottle full of fun and giggles.

What's It All About: Who knows? It's just a whole lotta fun.

What Brit Says: "Sometimes I forget how much I love this song, because it was the first one I recorded. I just think it's the coolest."

Grade: A+ This reggae-inspired track is guaranteed to get you out on the dance floor. We defy anyone to resist its catchy hook and pounding drumbeat.

● ● ● ● ● ● ● ● ● ● ● ● ● ● ● ● ● ● ●

TRACK 5: "BORN TO MAKE YOU HAPPY"

Written By: Kristian Lundin and Andreas Carlsson

Produced By: Kristian Lundin in Stockholm, Sweden

Tempo: Mid-tempo, a swingy song you can dance to.

What's It All About: A broken romance leaves our heroine pondering life without the object of her affection. She eventually realizes she needs to move away from "a dream of you and me."

What Brit Says: "I like the message of this song. It lets people know it's possible to move on, no matter what."

Grade: A+ The music of a mesmerizing keyboard draws you into the world of lost love and loneliness. Its plaintive chorus should inspire the weepies in anyone with an unfulfilled crush.

• • • • • • • • • • • • • • • • • • •

TRACK 6: "FROM THE BOTTOM OF MY BROKEN HEART"
Written By: Eric Foster White
Produced By: Eric Foster White in New York City, NY
Tempo: Power ballad deluxe.
What's It All About: A serious tearjerker, this is another song about a love that's been left behind. The girl in the song is begging her beloved to rekindle the fire between them, telling him that he is her "first love" and "true love." Whether he agrees or not is yet to be seen.
What Brit Says: "There's something about a sad love song that really gets to me."
Grade: A++++ The highest grade possible. This song elegantly blends Brit's powerhouse vocals with a lyric that's bound to break your heart. It's a perfect showcase for her awesome talent, a ballad that will bring a tear to the eye of anyone who's ever been in love.

• • • • • • • • • • • • • • • • • • •

TRACK 7: "I WILL BE THERE"
Written By: Max Martin and Andreas Carlsson
Produced By: Max Martin and Rami in Stockholm, Sweden
Tempo: Slow to mid, a song you and your friends can sway along with.
What's It All About: Britney asserts "I'll Be There" for the one she loves—but the song is

also appropriate to sing to a best friend. It's a song of loyalty, trust, and the bonds and strength of friendship.

What Brit Says: "I think this is the best thing you could ever say to a friend."

Grade: A++ So catchy it'll carry you away. (We definitely think this song has the makings of a summer smash!) This is the kind of song you'll want to dance to with your true blue best buds.

• • • • • • • • • • • • • • • • • • • •

TRACK 8: "I STILL LOVE YOU"

Written By: Eric Foster White

Produced By: Eric Foster White in New York City, NY

Tempo: Power ballad.

What's It All About: A loving duet with male vocalist Don Philip, this song is a joint declaration of the truest love—both croon, "You are my summer breeze . . . my autumn touch of love . . . my sky, my rain . . ."

What Brit Says: "I really enjoyed singing with Don—I think our voices sound really nice together."

Grade: A+ An anthem of love, this song is destined to become a favorite for couples. This is definitely a perfect "first dance" song, one you'll want to share with someone very special.

• • • • • • • • • • • • • • • • • • • •

TRACK 9: "THINKIN' ABOUT YOU"

Written By: Mikey Bassie and Eric Foster White

Produced By: Eric Foster White in New York City, NY

Tempo: Mid-tempo, another swaying song.

What's It All About: We're back in familiar territory, with a lovestruck lady who just can't stop thinking about her boyfriend. But rather than sounding forlorn, our Ms. Britney sounds perfectly content to spend those "days thinkin' about you."

What Britney Says: "I always like singing about relationships, but since I travel so much, I don't have one right now. Still, I know what it's like to spend all day thinking about someone."

Grade: B+ This one's not as intense as "(You Drive Me) Crazy," but it still has enough of that infectious, dancing beat to make it a winner.

• •

TRACK 10: "E-MAIL MY HEART"

Written By: Eric Foster White

Produced By: Eric Foster White in New York City, NY

Tempo: Mid-tempo, yet easy to dance to.

What's It All About: Something all Nineties ladies can relate to—a girl sends her loving wishes and apologies to a crush who's hit the road. The catch of course—she's sending those messages via E-mail, and she's patiently waiting for him to send one back to her.

What Brit Says: "Anyone with a computer can relate to this one, I think."

Grade: A Looks like true love in cyberspace—Britney's quivery, moving vocals wrap around the lyrics and create a song that's timely in its technology, but timeless in its emotion.

• •

TRACK 11: "THE BEAT GOES ON"
Written By: Sonny Bono
Produced By: Eric Foster White in New York City, NY
Tempo: Up-tempo, funk-a-dellic, and totally retro.
What's It All About: This funky, bouncy tune is a remake of a song that was a smash hit for Sonny and Cher back in the late Sixties—ages ago! It's basically a song that says, "Time passes, so what?"
What Brit Says: "This song was the greatest fun to do. It has a real retro sound I think people will like a lot."
Grade: B Not the best song on the album, but "The Beat Goes On" is a whole lot of hippy, happy fun. The funky background sound effects help a lot, and of course, Britney's voice is right on the money. Throw on those bell-bottoms and turn up the tunes!

chapter eleven

Britney Makes Her Mark

While Britney was recording her album, no one could have predicted the huge success she would have with it. Although everyone who heard it agreed that she had the right stuff—that her voice was strong, clear, and true—a question still remained: Would Britney make it to the very top?

The forecast looked good. Hanson, the Backstreet Boys, 'N Sync, 5, and 98° had opened the door, and pop music had walked right in. On every radio throughout the country and on MTV and VH1, it was pop music that audiences wanted to hear. That audience—the teen audience—had embraced the happy, perky tunes, the sweet love ballads, and the peppy lyrics offered by the boy pop-meisters. Would Britney, as a female, also find a home in the pop music world?

The answer, of course, was a resounding yes! Girl fans, more than ready to embrace a voice of their own, took Britney in and supported her in a big way. GBritney's good looks and sweet, bubbly personality, but they too were listening to the cool tunes. Britney found herself in an incredible position—her single and her album both hit the number one position on the charts simultaneously—a feat not seen since 1992, when kid rappers Kris Kross did it with their debut. "I hoped and dreamed I would have a number one album," Britney told the *New York Post.* "But I never honestly expected it to happen."

Two years before, Britney had been living with her family and friends in a small town in Louisiana. Now she had pulled off an astonishing accomplishment, with the help of teens yearning for her brand of pop music. And you can bet that the media—newspapers, TV and radio stations, and magazines across the country—wanted to talk about it.

National magazines, like *Time* and *Newsweek,* may have thrown compliments Britney's way, but they remained somewhat skeptical about her staying power. *Time,* for example, compared her with eighties pop singer Tiffany—a solo artist whose career slowed down in the U.S. after only one hit. Britney acknowledged the musical comparison but scoffed at the suggestion that her career would be a short one. "We're two totally different people and our sound is totally different," she said.

Newsweek attributed Britney's quick climb up the ladder to the success of the guy groups who came before her, saying she'd "capitalized on two trends at once." *Newsweek* further stated that Britney "has the same cool, sexy style as such bubble-gum groups as the Backstreet Boys. But she's also a teenage girl singing about love in the mold of R&B singers Brandy and Monica."

While some in the media focused on examining Britney's music, others began to take a look at the general pop music phenomenon, which began with the debut of Hanson in 1997. Stan Goman of Tower Records told *USA Today,* "The record companies finally woke up to the fact that they had nothing the teenagers wanted. Now they have some teen stuff out there and it's great."

Of course, every popular movement has its detractors. There were even some people who weren't excited about Britney's music—or the new pop music culture that was so present on the radio. One radio consultant told *USA Today,* "A lot of these records are starting to sound alike. The songs might be testing well, but there's bound to be a backlash eventually." Sean Ross, editor of *Billboard*'s radio magazine, *Airplay Monitor,* was quoted as saying, "Some radio stations have a rule that only one teen act at a time can be in heavy rotation."

If Britney was disillusioned or discouraged by any of the reports, she certainly didn't show it. Truth is, she probably didn't have time to read them. She was way too busy! She appeared as a presenter on the American Music Awards, introducing the Goo Goo Dolls, one of her favorite bands. (She told the *Times-Picayune,* "I love the Goo Goo Dolls, but I was so nervous. All those eyes are on you—and to make it even worse, I was the only one who was out there by myself!") She was also appearing on TV talk shows like *Donny & Marie, The Ricki Lake Show,* and *The Howie Mandel Show*. Everywhere she went, she charmed people with her modesty and her sweetness.

And then, of course, there were the teen magazines, which were all totally delighted to devote endless pages to Britney and her boppin' good-time music. *Teen People* even treated Brit to a fashion makeover, dolling her up in a stunning gown that gave her an ethereal, angelic quality. Britney was floored by the attention. "It's so flattering, all these people doing all this for you," she said.

There are dozens of reasons for the negative views expressed by some critics regarding pop music, but the bottom line is this—the music most beloved by younger fans has *never* been taken seriously! If you do your research, you'll learn that the most important group in modern music history, the Beatles, also faced criticism in their early years. It wasn't until they entered their "experimental" phase that they began to receive unanimous praise. Pop music, with its happy-go-lucky lyrics and boppin' melodies, is often dismissed as "fluff," music without substance, by critics who take pleasure in their own nastiness.

Also, after many years of grunge and alternative music, critics began to equate "good" music with "angry" music. To them, Britney's brand of busting-good-time music seemed totally alien.

But Britney proved them all wrong, and it looks as if her smile-a-minute music is here to stay. With her enthusiasm, energy, sweetness, and talent, Britney's managed to win fans wherever she goes.

Although there will always be pessimistic people determined to tear down popular artists, the fact remains that Britney's music is a hit with her fans. And her warm personality is a hit with everyone.

chapter twelve

The Personal Side of Britney

What's Britney like behind the glitz, the glamour, and the bright lights? It might surprise you to know exactly how much like you she really is!

Britney in Person

Meeting Britney in person is every fan's dream. And everyone who's ever met her reports the same thing—she's absolutely the most down-to-earth, friendly, sweet girl you've ever had the pleasure to know.

Away from the spotlight, Britney is as natural as they come. She speaks with a soft, lilting Louisiana drawl, and her conversation is sprinkled with little Brit-isms, like "Oh my goodness." She constantly calls herself a "goob"—slang for a goofy kid. And she laughs and giggles like crazy.

Britney's all girl, and she loves doing what she calls "girly" things. Number one on that list is shopping—Brit's totally at home at the mall, and she loves spending her time looking through all the latest trendy fashions. She definitely likes trying on new styles—although the clothes she actually buys tend to be comfy rather than fashionable.

Britney also loves experimenting with her makeup and her hair, but when she's done, she quickly washes it all off and ties her locks into a simple ponytail. In fact, being able to look natural is one of the reasons Britney likes New

York City so much. "It's true what they say about New York," she told *Teen Beat*. "No one cares what you look like! If you need to run out and get something to eat, all you have to do is grab a jacket. At home in Kentwood, I would never leave the house unless my hair was just right. But I really like being able to just look natural when I'm not working."

Britney grimaces when she remembers her early makeup experiences—she started wearing makeup when she was fifteen, but she'd been experimenting for years, ever since she'd appeared on the *Mickey Mouse Club*. "When I was fifteen I'd put on that natural glow makeup you buy at the drugstore, and I had my lip gloss," she told *16* magazine. "I thought I was decked out! But now, I look forward to washing it off, not putting it on."

If you met Britney, you might be surprised at how natural she is! "At home, on the road, I never wear makeup, my hair's always tied back, and I'm always in sweats," she told *BOP* magazine. "If a photographer ever got ahold of me, he'd really be surprised!"

Finally, once you got to know Britney, you'd realize that she truly is astonished by all the success she's achieved. She's still the same modest, sweet, unspoiled girl she was before fame and fortune hit hard. "It's weird when people talk to me and act like I'm something so special," she told *16*. "I don't feel any different at all."

Britney at Home

When Britney returns home to Kentwood, she enjoys doing all the normal things she did before fame came calling. These days, she only gets to visit the folks at home every few months or so. The visits are brief but filled with activity.

When she gets home, the first thing she does is plop down on the daybed in her bedroom. "My room is such a girly room," she says. "I collect dolls, so my dolls are everywhere. I have these porcelain collectible dolls, and my *Little Women* dolls are everywhere. I also collect angels. And pictures galore! I have a small room, but it's cute. It's got a blue carpet and a white beanbag chair and a daybed, and of course my stereo and all my CDs. It's the perfect place for me to relax."

After about five minutes of relaxing, Britney's ready to spend some time with the family. Most times they just sit around the dining room table. "I get this major appetite when I get home," Brit admitted to *Tiger Beat* magazine. "My mom cooks baked chicken for me, which is one of my favorites."

Britney also enjoys spending time with her sibs, and when she returns home, hanging with them is the first order of business. "My sister's into sports," she told *SuperStars*. "I did think my sister would be interested in singing—she totally sings like I did when I was younger. But if you tell her to learn a song, she says, 'NO!' Then she picks up a baseball bat. She's a tomboy and she'll tell you exactly what she thinks all the time.

"And my brother, we just talk a lot. He's a great guy. He's a total country boy—he loves football and stuff like that. And he's totally into bodybuilding. He wants to get involved with orthopedics someday—oh yeah, he's a total sports guy!" To prove it, Britney might show you all the awards and trophies displayed on the entertainment center in the living room—that's where her mom and dad keep all the plaques, statues, and cups their brood has brought home.

After hanging with her family, it's time to meet up with her friends, many of whom she's kept since grade school. "We go to the show—the movies, we hang out, we have fun," she told America Online. "When I'm with my friends, I'm totally myself. We never talk about the music business. We mostly talk about them."

After Brit and her friends pack it in, Britney returns home to share girl-talk with her very best friend, her mom. "My mom is someone I can always talk freely to," she told *16* magazine. "There's nothing I can't share with her."

Then it's back to her bedroom, where Brit claims, "I conk out! My favorite way to relax is to take a bath and just go to bed and sleep."

Piggin' Out with Britney

Recently, while filming the video for her second single, "Sometimes," Britney dislocated her knee—while she was kicking up her right leg, her left knee gave out. The video shoot was postponed, and Britney got an unscheduled vacation. Guess what she wanted to do with her time off? "I wanted a good fattening sandwich," she told *Newsweek* magazine. "I went to Jack in the Box and just ate."

So now the truth is out—Britney loves to eat! Her secret is simply this: "I don't overdo anything. I just eat what I want, but I don't go crazy."

Britney also keeps herself in shape with serious exercising. She tries to maintain a fitness regimen on the road, although she admits her current schedule makes that difficult. "When I was recording the album, I used to do fifty sit-ups a night. And I was living in New York City, where you can walk everywhere, and that's great exercise. But with all this traveling, I don't have as much time to exercise. When I'm not doing anything else, I'm sleeping."

The rigors of performing do tend to keep Britney in shape—anyone's who's seen her on stage knows it's quite a workout. "Dancing has always been my favorite way to keep in shape," she told *Teen Machine* magazine. "I love to dance so much. I even try to keep up with classes when I can. There's no better way to stay toned and in shape—and it's so much fun, you forget you're doing something good for yourself."

Lookin' for Love

Like most young girls, Britney dreams about meeting the perfect guy one day. And she's very clear about what qualities constitute the perfect guy. "I'm looking for someone who's cute and funny and sweet, who'll totally support what I do," Britney told *16* magazine. "I want to meet someone who's confident, someone who's happy with themselves. And trust and honesty—those are the two most important things. In friendships and in love, trust and honesty are the foundations."

Britney knows that she might meet that special person anywhere—he might even be a fan! "If I met a person, and I liked that person—I guess he wouldn't be a fan anymore, he'd be a friend," she told America Online.

On the Road Again

The one place Brit is spending most of her time these days is on the road. Traveling the world in a bus or on a plane can make anyone homesick, and Britney is no exception. "I try to remember, the bus is sort of my home-away-from-home," Brit told *Teen Beat*. "But I can't really bring too much on the road. So I always keep my prayer book with me. It goes everywhere with me. It reminds me of home and keeps me centered and focused on what's important." That prayer book is never far away. "I always end the day with a prayer," she told *16* magazine. "It helps me sleep better."

When she's traveling, Britney not only stays connected to her faith, she also stays connected to her body and health. In addition to working out whenever she can, she makes sure to take special care of her voice. She sips hot water with lemon or hot tea whenever it feels strained or sore. She also does vocal exercises to keep her voice strong.

Keepin' It Together

Wherever Britney is on any given day, she always remembers how important it is to take care of herself. To that end, you won't find Britney doing anything to hurt her body or her mind—no smoking, drinking, or drugs, ever. "If you don't take care of yourself, you won't have anything," Britney told *SuperTeen*. "Doing stupid things, like taking drugs or drinking—that's only going to mess up everything. I've lived so many of my dreams, why would I ever throw it all away?"

chapter thirteen

Brit Power!

Her Personal Message of Positive Power

One of the things that makes Britney Spears such a special teenager—aside from her awesome talent and rocket-to-the-stars success, of course—is her normalcy. Like you, Britney has spent the past few years growing up and going through the day-to-day trials and tribu-lations of life. Remember, her superstardom is a brand-new thing—she's spent lots of years just being a regular teenager and going through the same things you go through every day.

And even with her monster success, she's still a totally average girl who reacts to life just the way you would. Want a for-instance? How about the fact that she has a major thang for actor Ben Affleck. "He's so cute! And he doesn't have a girlfriend now, does he?" she asked the reporter for *Newsweek* magazine—who was busy doing a story on *her*!

Need another example? How about the time she met the Backstreet Boys for the first time and went positively ga-ga over Kevin Richardson? "He was so beautiful—he's prettier in person!" she told *Teen Beat* magazine. "I was like, oh my goodness, I didn't know what to say. He asked me if we'd met before, in Atlanta, and I was like, 'Oh, sure, of course.' And at that time I'd never even been to Atlanta, so I was a total stupid-head."

Yet Britney can hardly imagine anyone

being starstruck over her—although it happens every day. "Sometimes fans come up to me and totally don't know what to say," she told *16* magazine. "I just talk to them and act completely normal, the same way I'd talk to anyone else. I try to make people feel comfortable because I know how it is. But the funny thing is— whenever anyone comes over and talks to me, it always seems like I look so gooby. I always think—goodness, couldn't you have noticed me when I was looking a little better?"

One of the things Brit is comfortable about is passing along a positive message to her fans. She hopes she can share her experiences with her fans and her friends so they can avoid some of the mistakes and missteps she's made along the road she's traveled.

Of all the experiences Brit has shared with her fans, the one that really tugged at her heart was her last serious relationship. Although she never revealed the guy's name, it was clear she was serious about him when, in June of 1998, she said in an interview, "There's someone special I talk to at home. We have very big phone bills—when I was in Singapore, I made a collect call one night and one call was $150! That's bad—his parents flipped out. It's hard to maintain the relationship, though—we were really serious at one point, but now—I'm going to have to travel so much if I go on tour. So it's kind of sad."

The relationship was one of the most important aspects of Britney's young life. But when she talked about it, she was able to keep it in perspective, and she was happy to share her experiences with her fans. As she told *Teen Machine* magazine, "You fall in love, and suddenly you find yourself with this person twenty-four—seven and it starts getting ridiculous. This person starts telling you what to do and what not to do and you're totally like, 'Oh, you're right!' But then, something just clicked in me one day and I was like, 'What are you doing?'"

Once Britney began actively pursuing her career, she knew she had to make a decision about this particular relationship. Luckily for her, the decision came easily. "He would tell me I'd changed and I'd tell him that he was the one who changed," she told *16* magazine. "He started constantly asking me where I was and what I was doing. I mean, there I was, working like crazy, for hours and hours all day long. I'd come home and call him, and he'd start pressuring me, asking me where I'd been all day. And I was like, 'What do you think? I was working.' He really couldn't understand that you really do get in at four in the morning when you're doing a video shoot. Or that when you're gone all day, you really don't have time to talk on the phone, not even to your mom. All you want to do is go straight to bed. He couldn't understand that, and I couldn't explain it. But I shouldn't have had to explain it. You shouldn't have to apologize for working your butt off. You're like, 'Please leave me alone. . . .' And then you realize, hey, what am I doing? What am I saying? Why am I making excuses for doing the work I love so much?"

Looking back on the experience, Britney realizes that it taught her a serious lesson, which she's glad to share with her female fans—girls who might one day find themselves in similar situations. "I think that no matter how serious a relationship is, you need to be able to have fun and do your own thing," she told *Teen Beat* magazine.

That message—have fun and do your own thing—is one that Brit's taken to heart. Her positive feelings toward herself and her career have given her the strength to be totally true to herself. She gets her strength from her family, her friends, and her faith in God, and she uses her strength to put a positive spin on every aspect of her life.

Fans might look at Britney and think, "Well, she has everything in the world to be positive about, doesn't she? She's famous, beautiful, talented, and she's meeting fabulous people every day. She's also living her dream and doing exactly what she wants to do!" But Britney is able to use her positive thinking power no matter what's going on in her life. And on the days when she's feeling less than wonderful, she always knows she can draw on her inner strength and confidence. "I always try and remember that everything is going to be all right, as long as I stay grounded and remember that I'm surrounded by love. My family, my friends, and now my fans give me so much strength," she told *All-Stars* magazine.

Britney's also a very strong believer in Girl Power (you remember, the kind the Spice Girls used to talk about!), and she translates that power into the simple advice she passes along to fans every day—fans who dream of one day becoming a singer just like Britney. "You've got to work hard and believe in yourself," Britney told America Online. "For me, it's such a great feeling, knowing that people have bought my album and like what I'm doing. But it's also important for people to like what they're doing. It's important to enjoy every minute of life. Whether it's singing you love, or sports or writing or whatever. You've just got to have faith in yourself, and believe you can do it."

Without Peers

Like most teenagers, Britney is well aware of the problem of peer pressure. She knows that teens face a lot of it, and she herself has had to deal with it from time to time. But Britney also knows that at the end of the day, the last person you see in the mirror is you, and she would never want to do anything to jeopardize her future. That means she stays true to herself. "I know it's hard, when your friends are telling you to try this or that," Britney told *SuperStars* magazine. "But it's very important for each individual to decide what's important to them, and then for each person to live their life based on that decision. I know that I always have to be true to myself, so when something comes up, and it's not right for me, I know it immediately."

Down But Not Out

Sometimes life throws a curve ball to even the brightest superstar. While filming the video for her second single, "Sometimes," Britney had a bad fall and twisted her knee. Although she took some time off to recuperate, staying off her feet to avoid inflicting more injury on the knee, it eventually became clear that she was going to need more help than just a little rest and relaxation could give. When she finally went into Doctors Hospital in New Orleans, Dr. Tim Finney—who's the chief physician for the New Orleans Saints football team—removed a one-inch piece of loose cartilage from her knee.

Britney was a little upset that the full extent of the injury hadn't been discovered right away, but she was pleased that the surgery went well and was determined to get back in dancing shape as soon as possible. She began working daily with a physical therapist who exercised the leg to keep it strong. She also began working out more seriously with hand weights, using them to strengthen her upper body and cardiovascular system. For several weeks, she used a pair of crutches to help her get around. "I get frustrated because when I go to make a public appearance, I can't dance," she told *16* magazine. When she filmed the "Walt Disney Easter Parade Special" in MGM Studios, she needed a golf cart to take her around the park, and when it came time to perform, she had to stay seated on a large chair while she sang ". . . Baby One More Time" to a crowd of screaming fans.

Britney sent the following message out to her fans, who were so concerned and worried (especially after hearing nasty Internet rumors suggesting that she might never dance again): "I want to thank my wonderful fans and all of the people who have offered their love and support during this time."

As you might have expected, the injury didn't keep her down. Before long she was back on her feet and moving to the beat—one more time!

chapter fourteen

Special
Fan
Section!

How to Reach Britney

Snail Mail

Britney Spears Fan Club
P.O. Box 250
Osyka, MS 39657

Britney absolutely loves getting fan mail—she says she does her best to get to as many letters as possible. Be sure and include a photo of yourself—it makes a letter much more personal. Also, if you include a self-addressed, stamped envelope, you're more likely to receive a reply. To really get your letter noticed, use pretty baby-blue colored stationery. It's her favorite, so it'll attract her attention. And don't stress out if you don't get a reply right away—be patient. You know Britney's schedule is demanding, and she really doesn't want to disappoint you.

E-Mail

Britney@peeps.com

Britney checks in with her E-mail as often as she can, although she admits she gets a little slack when she's away on tour. E-mail is an easy way to get connected to Britney.

Britney on the Web

The Internet is absolutely loaded with opportunities to chat with other die-hard Britney devotees. The official Britney Web sites are:

http://www.peeps.com/Britney
http://www.asylum.com/music

There are dozens of alternative sites to check out as well; here are just a few of the best ones (For easy access to these sites, you'll want to begin with a search engine like Yahoo or Dogpile. Type in the name Britney Spears, and you'll be in the loop):

- wallofsound.go.com/artists/britneyspears/ home.html
- reach.to/britney
- www.geocities.com/SunsetStrip/Stadium/ 7135/
- www.geocities.com/Hollywood/Agency/ 1951/Britney.html
- listen.to/britney_spears
- www.angelfire.com/hi2/britspears/britney. html
- come.to/britneyspearsaz

Web Pages

There are also over 850 Britney Web Pages out on the Internet. These Web Pages, usually created by fans for fans, are a great way to reach out and chat with Web friends. But be warned: These Web Pages are un-official, and often include information that is outdated, unsubstantiated, and downright untrue. Log on at your own risk. And definitely don't believe everything you read on the Web!

Britney Online

Britney often drops in at America Online to participate in chats with her fans—check out AOL for info on upcoming Britney events.

You can also post messages to Britney through AOL at keyword: Britney.

BE FOREWARNED! Britney *never* goes into chat rooms on her own! Although she loves participating in Online chats, it's always through America Online. If you're chatting somewhere else, and someone claims to be Britney Spears—don't believe it, 'cause it's not true!

Britney Facts at Your Fingertips

Real Full Name: Britney Jean Spears
Nickname: Brit
Birthday: December 2, 1981
Family: 'Rents are Lynne and Jamie, her big brother, Bryan, is 21, and her sweet sister, Jamie Lyn, is 8.
Pets: She's got a Rottweiler named Cain.
Height: 5'5"
Hair: It's dark blond, but when the light hits it a certain way, it can look almost strawberry blond.
Eyes: Brown

FAVORITES
Music: Mariah Carey, Prince, Aerosmith, Backstreet Boys
Sport: Basketball, swimming, gymnastics
Color: Baby Blue
Food: Pasta, hot dogs, and ice cream (specifically cookie dough flavor)

Hobbies: Shopping, watching movies (especially romantic comedies), and reading trashy romance novels.
Disney Character: Goofy
Walt Disney World Ride: Space Mountain
Cereal: Cocoa Puffs
Signature Saying: Britney often interjects her sentences with "Oh goodness!"
Wears: Tommy Hilfiger

Basic Britney—How You Can Look Like Her!

So, you say you want to capture Britney's unique and totally trendy look. It's not as tough as you might think—here are some basic steps you can take if you want to look just a little bit like Britney.

Hair

Britney likes to wear hers straight and long. She keeps her bangs trimmed so they just brush her eyebrows. The next time you get your hair cut, ask for a style that frames your face. For a night out, Brit might crimp her hair to achieve a wavy, mussed look. And these days, she's also in to wearing extensions, which add supersensational volume to her straight hair. If you can't afford extensions, you can crimp like a pro using a curling iron—all it takes is a little practice and patience, and you can achieve the amazing, full-bodied Britney look you love.

To protect her hair from the sun, Brit likes wearing baseball caps and hats. You should get into that habit as well, especially when the summer sun is really blazing down.

Makeup

No lie—Britney really doesn't like wearing too much of it when she's just hanging out. That could be because she has to slap on so much of it for her stage performances. For your best everyday Britney look, keep it simple:

• Start with a matte foundation that perfectly matches your skin tone. Apply with a sponge to keep the foundation from looking thick. Blend downward, toward your jaw. When the foundation is totally blended into your skin, reach for a light matching power and top the foundation off so it doesn't look wet or shiny.

• Brush a mauve or light pink blush on the apples of your cheeks. Blend the color in to avoid a streaky line. Using a huge blush brush, add touches of color to your temples and jawline—that'll pull it all together beautifully.

• Line your eyes with a simple dark brown pencil. (Use taupe or gray if your eyes are very light.) Speckle the pencil along your lash line to avoid a sharp, harsh line. To get Britney's look, *never* use liquid eyeliner, or colors like dark blue or purple.

• Use a brown-black mascara—one coat will keep the clumps away.

• Brown, mauve, pale purple, and pink—feminine and natural are the adjectives to remember when selecting eye shadow. To achieve Britney's look, brush a neutral shade on your lid, with a lighter, complementary shade on the brow.

• For full, Britney-bright lips, line yours with a pencil. Stay in the pink, peach, and mauve family (never any reds or dark browns!) Fill in with matte lipstick. For a natural everyday look, stick to lip gloss in a fresh, fun flavor.

• Keep your look natural at all times, and stay away from any makeup that leaves you looking shiny or garish. Fresh, clean, and natural is the way Britney likes to look every day.

For Nighttime Sizzle!

When Britney heads out for a night on the town, she adds a little more sparkle to her makeup with—glitter, naturally! And you can get the same look with a minimum of fuss. Apply your regular makeup, then accent with glitter and sparkles—use eye shadows and blush that have glitter blended right in. Nighttime is also the right time for brighter colors, so be sure and use a hotter pink lipstick to really add some pizzazz!

• For an all-over extrasensational look, use body glitter on your shoulders and arms. And don't forget to glitter up your hair a little—all the better to catch the bright night lights!

Clothes

Tommy Hilfiger, Betsey Johnson, Bebe—when Brit's out on the town, she loves dressing up in designer duds. (Britney is one of Tommy Hilfiger's models for Tommy Jeans—you may have already seen her in his ad campaign, along with singers Mya and Q-Tip.)

Out of the limelight, Britney is into comfy, trendy, casual, and cute outfits. She loves miniskirts with little T-shirts; rolled-up jeans and short-sleeve, scoop-neck sweaters; sneakers, sandals, and, of course, her beloved platform shoes. Basically, Britney likes to wear current fashions without getting too way-out. And she likes her clothes to fit properly—you'll never catch her in anything tight, because she loves to be comfortable.

On stage, it's a different story. Under the spotlight, Britney appears in short, midriff-revealing tops, baggy, low-hanging pants, and Skechers. But that's showbiz! When she's performing, Brit needs to be comfortable, but she also wants to catch the eye.

Britney also tends to change her look depending on where she is. When she's at home, she likes to look as natural as possible, but when she's up in New York City working on her music, anything can happen. "Things I would wear in New York I would never wear at home," she told Teen People magazine. "People at home would look at you and think you were crazy. In New York, you can walk out with purple hair and it doesn't matter." Not to worry, though—Brit totally bagged the idea of dying her hair purple!

• To get that Britney look: Team up baby Ts (in Britney's favorite color, baby blue) with denim mini-skirts and platform sandals. Or wear a short-sleeved cotton shirt over slick Capri pants. You also might check out those adorable knit tank tops that look so super over faded, wide-legged jeans.

• You don't have to spend a lot to look like Brit! Check out vintage clothing stores for adorable Capri pants, baby Ts, and even platform shoes.

• A Britney Fashion Factoid: Britney loves the way Jennifer Love Hewitt and Friends star Jennifer Aniston dress. She calls them her fashion icons.

Jewelry

Again, simplicity is key. Britney loves silver rings and necklaces, and drop earrings. She's also into arts-'n'-craftsy type jewelry—things that look handmade, like beads and Puka shells. She definitely avoids flashy stones, and she's totally *not* into piercing anything other than her earlobes.

Accessories

To pull it all together, Britney loves pulling on a hat—baseball caps, floppy hats, berets, she loves them all. She also loves fashionable belts, kneesocks, and backpacks (she really loves the see-through, balloon styles that are all the rage now). Finally, no Britney 'do would be complete without those adorable clip barrettes—Britney likes the sparkly ones shaped like butterflies. When it comes to accessories, the thing that Brit looks for is fun as well as fashion—she's willing to take a risk and try out something new and funky.

A Britney Must!

Brit loves painting her toenails! Her favorite colors are vampy rusty reds and the palest of pinks. It's a must for all the strappy sandals Britney wears during the summer months!

Doin' the Britney Workout

Take one look at Britney, and you'll know the girl is totally into staying in shape. And she doesn't starve herself either—that's something she knows is completely uncool. "I love to eat," she confesses. "And I love really fattening things. I love Southern food, like fried chicken and barbecue and mashed potatoes—I don't deny myself anything I love!"

So how does she keep herself in prime

baby T condition? Well, as you can imagine, performing every night helps. When you're on stage, under hot lights, dancing up a storm, it's easy to sweat off a few pounds! "It's a complete workout, believe me," Brit told *16* magazine. "You're constantly moving, sweating, and dancing—it is strenuous beyond belief."

But in addition to her on-stage athletics, Britney believes in maintaining a healthy exercise program—and you can, too! Just turn on your Britney CD and let the music move you. It's time to get those muscles toned and that heart pumping!

Step One—Warm It Up!

Brit knows it's important to never ever rush into exercising. Without stretching out your muscles, you're bound to end up with a painful cramp or worse. So do your warm-ups!

1. Stretch and breathe! Take deep breaths and fill your lungs with oxygen. As you breathe, raise your arms up and bring them down.

2. Stretch those legs! Do slow leg lunges to stretch out those muscles in the backs of your legs.

3. Move around! Get that blood pumping! Run lightly in place to loosen yourself up. Or better still, dance around like crazy. As Britney says, dancing vigorously is an excellent way to exercise. It'll really get that heart rate up!

The Workout
Sit-Ups

They're yucky, but Britney swears by them. One hundred of them every night! Be sure and practice proper posture so you don't hurt your back. Here's how:

• **Lie on the floor.** Place your hands on the sides of your neck, lightly. Spread your legs shoulder-width apart and bend your knees.

• **Sit up slowly.** Let your abdomen, not your back or neck, do the lifting.

• **Crunch it.** Bring your torso up off the floor, but don't sit all the way up. Just that slight movement will give you that "crunch" you're looking for.

• **Bring it on down.** Return to your original position slowly, with no jerking motions. Keep your movements fluid.

Leg-Lifts

• **Lie on your side.** Use your arms to keep yourself upright. Extend your legs and point your toes.

• **Lift.** Raise your leg slowly to a count of eight, until it is pointing toward the ceiling.

• **Lower your leg** to a count of eight.

• **Repeat 16 times.** Then flip over and do the other side.

Weights

To keep her arms looking buff and toned, Britney works out with weights. And don't let the concept of weights scare you—they won't turn you into Ms. Arnold Schwartzenegger! Two light (2½-pound) dumbbells are all it takes.

• When you're out doing your power walk, carry one dumbbell in each hand. It makes your workout even more powerful.

• Lift 'em! Hold the weights in your hands and bend your elbows. Lift one arm to the sky eight times, then lift the other eight times. Do three repetitions of this exercise.

Walk It!

Walking is much better—for you and your knees!—than jogging or running. Grab your Walkman, pop in a Britney tape, head to the park, and just walk. Keep a good pace—this isn't strolling time—but don't kick it up a notch to a jog. Listen to ". . . Baby One More Time" and just walk to the beat.

Staying Active

One of the best ways Britney knows to stay in shape is to stay active—to do the things you love to do anyway! Want some examples? How about biking, swimming, roller blading, hiking, playing basketball—or any other sport—with your friends? All these activities help you burn calories while you're having fun. And if you can get a great big group of your best buddies to join you, you'll have a most excellent time!

One of Britney's favorite activities is swimming—it's a great way to tone up your muscles and keep your heart strong. But the key to staying active is to choose something you're really into. That way you'll do it every day.

Another activity Britney can't do without is in-line skating. She loves lacing up the skates and taking a spin around the park. Of course, she never forgets to gear up, and neither should you—always remember to strap on the wrist, elbow, and knee guards, and pull on a helmet.

Keep It Cool—Down!

No matter what kind of workout you've chosen, be sure to cool down after you're done. Cooling down simply means giving your body a chance to relax. Doing some deep breathing and some bending and stretching exercises will give your body a chance to cool down properly.

Some "Britney Workout" Tips

1. Don't overdo it! Exercise is supposed to make you feel great, not rotten. If you push yourself too hard, you're bound to end up with seriously sore muscles.

2. Don't get freaky about it! If you start obsessing about your workout, or if it starts becoming too much "work" and not enough

fun, it's time to cut down. Remember, if you enjoy what you're doing, you'll do it more often—and reap the healthy benefits.

3. Drink lots of water! Before, during, and after your workout, you'll need to replace the water you've sweated out of your body. Keep pouring the water in, and you'll get most excellent results out of your body. In fact, it's a good idea to drink tons of water each day no matter what you're doing. It'll make your skin look great and keep you feeling fine.

4. Do exercise when you're feeling blue. The burst of energy will make you feel better.

5. Do exercise to music—Britney's music will do very nicely!

Party On—Throw a Britney Bash with Your Friends!

Looking for a new, totally funky, and unique idea for your next best-buddy get-together? How about a Britney Bash? Here's how:

• Invite your favorite Britney-fan friends for a festive sleepover—your best friend, your cousin, the girl in science class—anyone who shares your love of Britney and her good-time music.

• Choose Brit's favorite tunes! To get your party in gear, crank up the music—and make it music Britney herself would completely get into. To get the room dancing, slide in a Backstreet Boys or Robyn CD; to mellow out, switch to Mariah Carey; to pick up the energy level, listen to Prince's *Purple Rain* soundtrack CD. And of course, keep ... *Baby One More Time* close to the CD player, and have a Britney sing-along whenever the mood strikes you.

• OK, now it's time to eat! If Britney was at your house, she'd tell you to throw some hot dogs on the grill and stock up on the cookie dough ice cream. And make sure to keep some healthy snack foods around—things like veggies and dip and fruit slices. Nothing too fancy—Britney likes basic, good-tasting food best.

• Girls just gotta have fun, and that's what you're going to want to do at your girly gala. What would Britney like to do with you and your friends? Well, you could rent a slew of movies, like *My Best Friend's Wedding*, *The Horse Whisperer*, *Titanic* (OK, so it's going to be a long night—make lots of popcorn), and *Steel Magnolias*, and laugh, cry, and snack out all night. Or you could crank up the tunes and dance till you drop. Another very cool idea—experiment with makeup and new hairstyles. You can try new colors on one another, or give your best friend that 'do you've been dying to try. Try out body glitter, temporary tattoos—anything that looks cool and new to you.

• Talk about guys! Just like you, Britney adores indulging in girltalk, especially about cute guys. She definitely wouldn't mind joining you in an all-night discussion about which

Backstreet Boy is the cutest. (She'll tell you she went totally loopy over Kevin, who she says is absolutely gorgeous in person.)

• Conk out and sleep. After all that activity, you'll certainly be ready for bed.

chapter fifteen

Pop Quiz

Could You and Brit Be Best Friends?

You're crazy about Britney's brand of pop music. You think she's one of the coolest singers you've ever heard. And of course, you can't get enough of her awesome album and her totally watchable videos.

But do you have what it takes to be Britney's absolute best friend? Do you share tastes in music, movies, and hobbies? What about values, ideals, and ambitions—think both you and Brit are in agreement? Well, there's only one way to find out—read this book, then take this little quiz and see if you've got what it takes to spend quality best-buddy time with Britney Spears.

1. You and Britney are getting ready to spend the afternoon together. What activity have you planned?

   a) A day at the movies—a romantic comedy or a major five-hankie tearjerker, if possible.

   b) Shopping at the local mall—although you might just do a lot of trying on and little actual buying.

   c) Hanging out in your room, experimenting with makeup and listening to music.

2. Britney's off on another awesome tour of the U.S. Do you . . .

a) Expect to be invited along—after all, you're her best friend!

b) Get resentful and annoyed—you hate it when she's gone for long periods of time.

c) Smile and tell her you'll be waiting to hear all about it when she gets back.

3. You know Britney is way close with those 'N Sync babes, Justin and J.C. Do you . . .

a) Grill her about the guys—are they dating anyone? Could she fix you up?

b) Constantly ask her to tell you stories from the road.

c) Cut Brit a break—when the two of you hang out, you've got other things to talk about.

4. You're buying Britney some CDs for her birthday. What do you purchase?

a) Mariah Carey, Prince, and that new Backstreet Boys album, as soon as it's available

b) Classical music or operas

c) You don't buy any—you figure she probably has plenty of CDs already.

5. You and Britney are busy studying—what subjects is she tutoring you in?

a) Square dancing

b) History and English

c) Math

6. You've got a brand-new boyfriend—how does that affect your relationship with Britney?

a.) It doesn't—best friends stay best friends, even when a guy comes into the picture!

b) It changes it slightly—you tend to spend most of your "girltalk" time chatting about him rather than the two of you.

c) It totally alters it—after all, you've got to spend all your free time with him, don't you?

7. You want to have a singing career just like Britney's. Do you . . .

a) Constantly ask her to help you get a record deal.

b) Ask her advice occasionally and really listen to what she tells you.

c) Assume Brit wouldn't want you as competition.

8. It's a beautiful afternoon and Britney has the day off. You both decide to . . .

a) Get active—swimming, a goofy game of one-on-one basketball, or a long walk in the park.

b) Get silly—go for a ride with the car top down, singing along to the radio.

c) Get lazy—pull out the lawn chairs and the sunglasses, mix up a pitcher of iced tea and lounge out.

9. Which song on ...*Baby One More Time* is Britney's favorite?

    a) "The Beat Goes On"

    b) "...Baby One More Time"

    c) "Soda Pop"

10. Your friends at school are gossiping about Britney and they urge you to tell them your secrets. You ...

    a) Reluctantly join in, telling a few stories and revealing a few confidences.

    b) Tell them no, your friendship with her means too much.

    c) Babble about everything the two of you did last weekend.

Answers

1. Trick question—all three activities would make Britney smile.

2. C. Traveling and touring are major parts of Brit's career—she'd want your support.

3. C. Are you her friend 'cause you like *her* or the 'N Sync guys?

4. A.

5. B.

6. A. Britney knows that friendships last forever, and she'd want to know you felt the same way, even if a new guy did enter the picture.

7. B. Brit's glad to answer your questions—just don't ask 'em every other minute!

8. Another trick question—any of the three would be excellent!

9. C. Brit's admitted to having a soft spot for "Soda Pop."

10. B. Loyalty is important to Britney, and she'd want to know she could trust you.

HOW'D YOU DO?

10 Matches: Total Girl Power!—You and Britney would definitely be buds forever.

7–9 Matches: Not Too Bad—You know a lot about Brit, and would probably get along famously with her.

4–6 Matches: Yikes! You and Brit don't have much in common besides great taste in music.

0–5 Matches: No way! Better read this book "one more time," 'cause what you don't know about Britney would fill a book of your own!

chapter sixteen

Britney's Ultrabright Future

With her talent, determination, and will to succeed, Britney Spears's star is destined to shine brightly for years to come. The only question is, will that star be shining in the music business or in movies and TV?

Although she's found fame as a pop singer extraordinaire, Britney's also been dabbling in acting, something she's been interested in since her early days in New York City, when she made her debut on the Off-Broadway stage in *Ruthless.*

In 1999, Britney appears in three episodes of the WB network's smash hit show *Dawson's Creek,* where she will help create a character for herself—a character that may eventually spin off into a TV show of her own! Although Britney's tour schedule is demanding—and sometimes overwhelming—she's working closely with Columbia Tri-Star Television, the studio that developed *Dawson's Creek* and *Party of Five.* Her entertainment lawyer, Larry Rudolph, told the *New York Post,* "Britney is developing a relationship with the top TV company for the type of series she might want to do." That means Britney might be ruling the TV airwaves very soon!

And although Britney's always remained focused on her music career, she's never been shy about reflecting on her future—a future that just might include acting. "I would definitely like to get into films," she told America Online.

"That would be fun! I've already done regional commercials and theater, so I have some experience. It would be an exciting thing, wouldn't it?"

It makes sense that Britney might want to explore other outlets for her abundant talents. After all, she's been quoted as admiring Madonna, who's known for her chameleon qualities—reinventing herself from pop icon to movie star whenever a good film role comes along. And Britney's voice has already been compared to Madonna's—a comparison Britney considers a great compliment. "I like being compared to Madonna, because I totally respect and admire her," says Britney. "She's grown so much as an artist, and she's always changing. I think she's an amazing artist." And she told *USA Today,* "I'd love to do a duet with Madonna 'cause she's just, like really out there. I think it would be a real shocker to everyone if we performed together."

There's no reason Britney couldn't become an equally amazing artist. And there's also no reason Britney won't eventually shock the world with her own awesome abilities. Everyone who comes into contact with her recognizes that she has something very special to offer the world. Jeff Fenster from Jive Records told *Billboard* magazine that Britney was "intriguing" and that her talent was "boundless." Nigel Dick, the director of her video, praised her ability in front of the cameras. And Barry Weiss of Jive Records told *USA Today* that Britney has "a real girl-next-door appeal. Every girl wants to be like her and every guy wants to get to know her."

But singing and acting aren't the only things in Brit's future. This bright young lady totally recognizes the importance of education, and she's looking forward to working out with her brainpower one day soon. "I do want to go to college," she told America Online. "Right now I'm focusing on my career, of course, but I definitely want something to fall back on. This business is crazy—you never know what's going to happen from day to day." There's no doubt that Britney will get her degree one day, perhaps majoring in her academic love, English. "There's so much I want to do in my life," she says. "I've got my whole life ahead of me, and I think if I put my mind to it, I can do anything!"

What the Stars Say about the Star!

If you ask Britney, she'll tell you that the future probably hinges more on hard work than horoscopes, but she's definitely one to keep an eye on the star signs. And according to Britney's charts, the future's so bright she's gonna have to wear serious shades!

Like many Sagittarians, Britney has diverse talents. The music, theater, and movie worlds are filled with stars born under this illustrious sign, like Brad Pitt, Katie Holmes, Kim Basinger, and Brendan Fraser. Blessed with candor and honesty, those born under the sign of the Archer tend to be straightforward and truthful, with a need to reach out and touch others. That could be why Britney is so inspired to touch fans with her music.

Britney also has the cheerfulness and friendliness often attributed to Sagittarians. That means that when the chips are down, she's got the positive and upbeat attitude it takes to keep forging ahead. There's no doubt she'd be able to move smoothly into the acting biz, but if things didn't go her way in the beginning, she'd still be able to keep a smile on her face anyway.

Acting often beckons to those born between November 23 and December 21. Sagittarians enjoy studying human nature, and they often have a good time playing different roles with their friends.

And finally, those born under this sign often say they feel lucky. Certainly Brit will tell you she feels lucky to be doing what she's doing. But the truth is, luck has little to do with it. Those born under this sign enjoy taking chances and plunging into new things with a lot of energy and enthusiasm. That's probably got more to do with Britney's success than something as hard to define as luck. The truth is that Britney's optimism and happy-go-lucky attitude, mixed liberally with her ambition and willingness to work hard, have combined to bring her to this point in her career.

And that means that whatever Britney wants to accomplish, she probably will!

Crowing for Britney!

In Chinese astrology, Britney was born (1981) in the year of the Rooster! This ancient mystic study, which dates back to the Ming Dynasty (which ruled China 350 years ago) holds that people take on the characteristics of the animal that governs their year of birth.

So what traits might Britney share with a rooster? Her singing calls up sunshine. Plus, people born under the sign of the Rooster tend to be very honest and straightforward—two qualities Britney definitely exhibits.

Rooster-year chicks also tend to be multi-talented and enthusiastic—certainly two more traits you could use to describe Brit. They do well in music and the arts because they really love to work hard at their craft.

Those born under the Rooster sign make excellent best friends because they are so loyal and devoted—if you want to share a secret with someone who absolutely won't tell, share it with a Rooster person! They also love to entertain and make people smile—two things Britney does every day!

What does the future hold for Britney using this method of astrology? Well, 1999 is the year of the Rabbit, and according to Chinese astrology, this year holds tons of positive changes for Roosters. It looks as if Britney's headed for more success, as well as big changes in her career (Hmm, could that acting gig on *Dawson's Creek* really be leading to big things? Looks like it, according to this chart). Keep your eye on Britney—1999 might just be her biggest year yet!

Romance, Romance

Britney's definitely a romantic at heart—you can hear it in her voice when she croons love songs like "Born to Make You Happy" and "I Will Still Love You." But her experiences have taught her to be careful when it comes to love and never to settle for someone who isn't absolutely right for her.

Britney wouldn't mind dating someone who worked in show business, and she certainly wouldn't refuse a date with someone tall, dark, and gorgeous. But she's learned that the most important things in a relationship are trust and understanding, and that a beautiful heart and soul are what really makes a guy a winner. So while she will always keep her eyes open for Prince Charming, she's not going to waste her time kissing any toads.

Right now, Britney's career is the most important thing to her. But she's keeping an open mind and an open heart, and she knows someday she'll find a guy who's perfect for her.

The Final Word

Whatever Britney does in her life, there's no way she'll completely give up her first love, music. After all the years she's spent working to get to the top, you can bet she'll never stray far from the one thing that makes her most happy. "I always knew this was what I wanted to do," she has said. "It's been a lot of work, but it's been absolutely worth it!"

JACKIE ROBB is a freelance writer based in the New York area. She also writes for a variety of teen magazines. She is currently working on several other books on young artists and performers, as well as a movie script and a play. She lives in New Jersey and is the biggest Britney fan who ever lived— besides you, of course!